302·5

COS

BULLYING AND HARASSMENT IN THE WORKPLACE

Dedication
This book is dedicated to all those
who tirelessly and relentlessly strive
to eradicate harassment from the workplace.

Lucy Costigan

Bullying and Harassment in the Workplace

A GUIDE FOR EMPLOYEES, MANAGERS AND EMPLOYERS

the columba press

First published in 1998 by
the columba press
55A Spruce Avenue, Stillorgan Industrial Estate, Blackrock, Co Dublin

Cover by Bill Bolger
Origination by The Columba Press
Printed in Ireland by Colour Books Ltd, Dublin

ISBN 1 85607 237 1

Author's Note
The case studies quoted in this book are based on actual people who have experienced bullying or harassment at their place of work in Ireland. To protect the anonymity and the livelihoods of all those who have kindly spoken to the author, some details of their work situation, as well as names and specific job-titles, have been changed.

Acknowledgements

Life is a mysterious winding path of chance/coincidence/destiny. This book would not have been written if my path had not connected with two quite remarkable individuals:

A million thanks, Frank, for being the inspiration, the advisor and the guide when I needed a steady hand to lead me through that corporate quagmire. As I've joked with you before: a lot can change in a year! I'm eternally grateful. I really appreciated your helpful advice during the writing of this book, the sharing of your vast experience, all that proof-reading, and your ocean of kindness.

Thank you, Margaret, for your solid friendship and support. Your courage, your indomitable spirit, and your unshakeable principles in the face of all adversity, have been to me beacons of light and hope.

To the Costigan-Cullen-McGovern clan:

Thanks Theresa, Anthony, and Val, for all your help with the research, and for your constant love and friendship.

Thank you Ray, for your meticulous and professional editing, and for all your candid advice.

Michael; a big 'thank you' for all your help with promotion, and for your wonderful photos.

To Paul and Sharon, 'the golden spirits': Thank you both for all the laughs, the pool games, the music sessions and for your unique friendship.

Thanks to Sean and Damien for your much appreciated support.

To each of the 'loves' of my life:

Thanks to Andrew, Carmel, Paddy, Isabel, Clara, Maura, and Phena, for your multi-dimensional stimulation! Hopefully there'll be more time now for those all-night talks, mouth-watering cuisine in Temple Bar, walks along the beach, tennis and picnics in Bushy, a few wild blues sessions, and some jet-setting around the globe!

Thank you Brendan, from the Irish Spiritual Centre, for a decade of encouragement, guidance and light.

Thank you Mary (Costin) and Rita for helping with the research of the book, and for your friendship.

Thanks to John O'Donoghue (Minister for Justice, Equality and Law Reform), Pat Murray (Minister's Personal Secretary), Frank O'Malley (SIPTU), Professor Joyce O'Connor and the library staff at NCIR, Peter Flood and Jenny Hayes (IBEC), Tom Wall (ICTU), Andrew Rea (G. C. McKeowns), Dr Richard Wynne (Work Research Centre), Dr Mona O'Moore (Anti-Bullying Centre), Vivette O'Donnell (Campaign Against Bullying), and the staff of the Employment Equality Agency, for the giving of your precious time and for your generous assistance.

A special thanks to all those who have spoken to me, and have granted me permission to include their personal experiences in the book.

Contents

Introduction

I met her on the Dublin to Wexford train. She was in her early forties, tall, dark shoulder-length hair, blue eyes, impeccably dressed. We chatted about the weather. Then she asked me 'What do you do – workwise, I mean?' I replied that I worked in private practice as a counsellor and psychotherapist. 'So you're used to dealing with broken people,' she said. 'Well, I'm sorry to say I must count myself among that group also.' She cast her eyes downwards. 'It's my work,' she said, by way of explanation. 'I work with a boss from hell!'

Over the next two hours Carla described the soul-destroying work environment in which she spent the major part of her waking life:

I'm in the civil service. I'm a secretary, and my boss has a very high-powered position. I can only describe him as two people, Jekyll and Hyde. Some days he comes in to the office all smiles, and tells me how much my new blouse suits me, and asks me how I enjoyed the weekend in Galway. If later that afternoon the bubble bursts, he'll criticise my every move, every letter I type, every meeting I arrange for him. Sometimes he'll shout, and the other girls will cower behind their desks, afraid that he'll pick on them next.'

I hate to admit it but I've cried in front of him several times. 'Women!' he said the last time I cried, and walked away, slamming the door behind him. I'm sure it feeds his ego even more to see me crying but I just can't help it. I feel so humiliated. The derogatory things he says about my work are so hurtful, after all the extra hours I work to get him out of a fix whenever he's snowed under. I feel about a foot high when he shouts at me. Like a child who's being chastised by her father. It's pathetic. It was all so different before he came. My previous boss was a real gentleman. I loved my work then. Now I hate it. I couldn't dare report him, though. He'd destroy me. And I don't want to leave because my salary is so

11

good. I'm just wishing my life away until retirement. Unless
– please God – maybe he'll be moved!
She started sobbing, then buried her face in her hands.

'Sorry!' she said. 'Once I start on about my work, it kind of
takes me over. Here I am, on my way to spend a weekend
with my sister, and I might as well be sitting at that cursed
desk. I suppose it has taken me over. I should really go for
counselling myself. I can't go on like this.'

The above is by no means an exception to the many cases of harassment in the workplace which I have come across in both my
personal and professional life. Harassment of any kind abhors
me. Immediately pictures spring to mind of the classic bully
who seeks to experience a momentary surge of power while
abusing and humiliating an isolated victim. Whether it be child
abuse, wife beating, rape, bullying in school, or harassment perpetrated in the workplace, the long term effects as experienced
by the abused can be both devastating and emotionally crippling.

Since the time of the industrial revolution, at the end of the
eighteenth century in Britain, workers have struggled to improve their often appalling and injurious working conditions.
The formation of trade unions, and the agitation for employment legislation over the last two centuries, has done much to
improve workers physical conditions. But what of workers' psychological conditions?

Over the last decade there has been a huge increase in public
awareness of the frequency with which other forms of abuse
occur, and the effects on those who have been abused. As a society we are only just coming to a vague awareness of the extent to
which harassment occurs in the workplace. It is my work as a
counsellor and psychotherapist which brings me face to face on
at least a weekly basis with sexual harassment, bullying, violence, and high levels of stress, as suffered by men and women
in the Irish workplace. It is this experience which has given me a
particular awareness of the extent of the problem, and the terrible effects on those who feel trapped and unable to pull themselves free of such abuse.

So when I write of harassment in the workplace I see before
me the faces of those I have met who have suffered: the forty-
five-year-old factory worker and father of four who can't stop
the tears flowing because of the way he's repeatedly criticised,
day after day, in front of his mates by a new boss; the eighteen-
year-old secretary who feels suicidal after she's been threatened

with dismissal unless she succumbs to the sexual demands of her sixty-year-old boss; the fifty-year-old woman who is ignored and isolated from co-workers by a policy of 'divide and conquer' as practised by a new manager.

My own experience of the workplace includes being employed as a trainee-accountant by a firm of accountants in Wexford Town, and as a computer programmer by a financial institution in Dublin. As a consequence of direct experience while working in Dublin, I joined SIPTU and became conscious of the importance of working towards an harassment-free workplace. I then went on to study 'lead management' and counselling, and became a member of the Institute for Reality Therapy in Ireland, and the Irish Association of Hypno-analysts. My work as a counsellor and psychotherapist has given me an even greater insight into the many problems which are experienced by employees when a' boss management' ethos is in operation, or when there is no policy in place to protect the psychological welfare of workers.

This book is written for employees, management and employers, to help raise the awareness that bullying and harassment does occur, and is occurring, in many work places in Ireland. It is also a guide for those who are experiencing harassment at work, to help them identify unfair and unlawful treatment, and to provide them with contact names and numbers where support and help can be obtained. It can also be used by those who are responsible for formulating work policies to help combat harassment at work, while boosting staff-management relations and productivity.

Comment from the
Department of Justice, Equality and Law Reform

In a letter to the author, dated 6 March 1998, the position of the Department of Justice, Equality, and Law Reform, regarding bullying and harassment in the workplace was stated thus:

> Responsibility for the problem of bullying in the workplace rests primarily with the Health and Safety Authority, an organisation under the aegis of the Department of Enterprise, Trade and Employment. However, the problem of sexual harassment in the workplace is provided for in the Employment Equality Bill, 1997, which is currently under consideration by the Oireachtas, and which is the responsibility of this department.

> For the first time in Irish legislation it is proposed to define sexual harassment and to set out the system of redress in such cases. This department also publishes a Code of Practice on Measures to Protect the Dignity of Men and Women at Work.

According to John O'Donoghue TD, Minister for Justice, Equality and Law Reform:

> It is important that action be taken to deal effectively with sexual harassment in the workplace not only because it is inherently unjust to its victims but also because it has an indirect negative effect on the working environment. It is something which should not be tolerated in any workplace and I hope that its inclusion in the new Employment Equality legislation will be instrumental in its elimination.

CHAPTER ONE

Definitions of harassment

The difficulty in adequately defining harassment
Before exploring the extent of harassment in the workplace, it is important to define the types of harassment which workers may be subjected to. Harassment is such a complex issue, and comes in so many shapes and forms, that it is extremely difficult to arrive at a concrete definition, one which is inclusive of all perspectives. Yet it is vital that we attempt to put a label on many workers' experiences, to help them understand what is happening in their workplace and causing them untold fear, stress and anguish.

Four types of harassment have been identified as occurring in the workplace: sexual harassment, bullying, violence, and stress. The boundaries of each type of harassment are anything but clearly defined. For example, sexual assault or rape is a definite case of sexual harassment, but it is also a violent crime. Verbal abuse is a definite case of bullying, but may also be classified as psychological violence. The person who suffers any form of harassment is always put under high levels of stress. Yet excessive levels of stress may also be due to unreasonable demands which are placed on an employee, such as being coerced into meeting unrealistic deadlines. These latter demands are often made in a threatening and bullying manner. When we look at harassment at work, the boundaries between each type of harassment may be blurred, but there are certain fundamental points which we must be aware of.

In the case of sexual harassment, we need to be clear that it is *not* acceptable social interaction in the workplace. It is very natural to feel attracted to a person we are working with, as we are all sexual beings. A feeling of attraction may add an extra spice to the working relationship, or liven up an otherwise routine work day. However, sexual harassment is *not* about attraction. It may often be misrepresented as sexually motivated behaviour, but research shows that it results primarily from an excessive need to dominate. It is the unwanted nature of sexual harass-

ment which distinguishes it from welcome and reciprocal attention. It may result from a lack of awareness of what sexual
harassment is, or from a complete disregard for the rights and
dignity of the person being harassed.

A perpetrator of sexual harassment cannot plead ignorance
as a defence. Women often feel uncomfortable and embarrassed
when men in an office start telling 'blue jokes', which portray
women as sexual objects. But where does one draw the line
between harmless office fun and sexual harassment? The difference is when a woman feels so upset and demeaned that she
can't face going to work, and suffers a loss of confidence as a result of such comments or 'jokes'. A useful guideline is to consider
the feelings of others.

Likewise we need to develop an awareness of which behaviours constitute bullying in the workplace. A once-off reprimand
by a manager, or a sharp or snappy comment from a colleague
does not amount to bullying. All human beings are fallible, and
perfect relations between all staff members, all of the time, are
not possible. Interpersonal or group conflicts can damage the
work environment, and can be a source of stress to those concerned, but this does *not* constitute bullying. In cases of bullying,
an individual is persistently criticised, humiliated, threatened,
or ridiculed. In some instances, the perpetrators may not even
realise the impact their behaviour is having on the victim. One
person's joke may be another person's nightmare. As with sexual
harassment, it requires some degree of sensitivity to what may
cause offence and what may be enjoyed as harmless fun.

Some behaviours are very obviously abusive, such as physical violence which is perpetrated against an employee, either by
colleagues, superiors, or members of the public. There are many
other behaviours, however, which are covert and insidious and
are more difficult to detect. These may include coercing employees
into striving to achieve impossible deadlines or objectives,
thereby causing staff undue and excessive stress. Manipulation
and intimidation may also be used to force workers into accept-
ing conditions which are highly stressful and injurious to their
mental health and well-being. Some degree of stress is experienced by all of us in the course of our daily lives. However, a
stressful working environment develops when there are inadequate safeguards and controls in operation, to protect workers
from incurring excessive and dangerous levels of stress.
Therefore, when we consider bullying we are apt to discover

many 'grey' areas, where behaviours may overlap into several types of harassment.

Up until 1998, there has been no legal definition of sexual harassment in Irish law, because it has not been specifically mentioned in any legislation. Pending legislation, which is due to be passed in the summer of 1998, will rectify this position by the introduction of a new Employment Equality Act. In the following sections I will give definitions for sexual harassment, bullying, violence and stress, as defined by leading organisations and unions in the area, and as defined by pending legislation.

Sexual Harassment
The Employment Equality Act 1977 (section 27) prohibits discrimination on grounds of sex in relation to conditions of employment. The term 'conditions of employment' is not defined in legislation, but in 1985 the Labour Court stated: 'freedom from sexual harassment is a condition of work which an employee – of either sex – is entitled to expect. The court will accordingly treat any denial of that freedom as discrimination within the meaning of the Employment Equality Act 1977.' (Labour Court Order EEO 2/85)

Sexual harassment is defined as 'unwanted conduct of a sexual nature or other conduct based on sex affecting the dignity of women and men at work.' (Resolution of the Council of Ministers (29 May 1990), and the European Commission code of practice on protecting the dignity of women and men at work (No 49/1, 24.2.92.).)

According to the Services, Industrial, Professional, Technical Union (SIPTU): 'Sexual harassment can be broadly described as persistent, unwanted sexual innuendoes, physical contact or propositions that are offensive to the person receiving this attention. It includes all forms of harassment from unpleasant remarks to sexual assault. More specifically, sexual harassment can include any of the following:
* Repeated and unwanted verbal or physical advances
* Sexually explicit or discriminatory remarks
* Unwelcome comments about personal dress or appearance
* Demands for sexual favours
* Offensive use of pin-ups, pornographic pictures, etc.
* Display in the workplace of material of an explicitly sexual nature, including computer software packages, for example.'
  (Sexual harassment is no joke)

The Irish Business Employers Confederation (IBEC) defines sexual harassment as 'conduct towards another person which is sexual in nature or which has a sexual dimension and is unwelcome to the recipient. Examples of harassment can include:

Verbal:
* Requests or demands for sexual favours
* Suggestive remarks
* Degrading abuse or insults
* Jokes or tricks of a sexual nature

Physical:
* Gesturing of a sexual nature
* Unnecessary touching
* Indecent exposure
* Actual assault, up to rape

Visual:
* Displaying pornographic material at the workplace.'
(Guideline 4: Dealing with sexual harassment in the workplace)

The Employment Equality Agency (EEA) gives the following definition for sexual harassment:
* Sexually suggestive jokes or comments
* Questions or insults about one's private life
* Lewd comments about physical appearance
* Unwelcome sexual attention
* Display of offensive material
* Leering, offensive gestures or whistling
* Groping, patting or unnecessary touching
* Suggestions that sexual favours may further someone's career, or that refusal may damage it.
(Sexual harassment and dignity at work)

The Rape Crisis Centre states that, because it can take may forms, sexual harassment is not easy to define. 'It can be both verbal and physical, range from a pointed personal remark to a sexually-explicit pin-up on an office wall, to serious sexual assault. It can assume the guise of a joke with embarrassing sexual overtones, or pressure to exchange sexual favours for career advancement.' It goes on to define sexual harassment as 'sexually-orientated behaviour which is both unwelcome, and unreciprocated, the effect of which is to embarrass, frighten, humiliate, or bully the victim.' *(Sexual harassment in the workplace)*

A person can be sexually harassed by someone of a higher, a similar, or a lower grade. Both women and men can find themselves being sexually harassed, though women are by far the majority of victims, and it can involve all classes and age groups. Sexual harassment can also be perpetrated by a member of the same sex. It is often the product of the dominance of the economically or professionally strong over the weak and defenceless. New employees, gay and lesbian workers, or those who are perceived as being in some way different are particularly vulnerable.

Sexual harassment can occur anywhere, at any time, either at work or outside of work, such as at an office party or when one member of staff is giving another a lift home. The employer is always liable where a case of sexual harassment has been proven. The employer's responsibilities extend to others with whom staff are interacting in the course of their work, such as customers, agents or patients.

Bullying

'Bullying at work constitutes offensive treatment through vindictive, cruel, malicious or humiliating attempts to undermine an individual employee or groups of employees. These persistent negative attacks on their personal and professional performance are typically unpredictable, irrational and often unseen.' *(IBEC: Guideline No 19)*

According to SIPTU, examples of bullying are:
* Aggressive behaviour by a manager, supervisor or colleague
* Repeated verbal harassment
* Personal insults and name-calling
* Persistent criticism
* Persistent picking on a person for the butt of jokes, horseplay, uncomplimentary remarks or other behaviour likely to cause offence
* The maligning or ridiculing of a person directly or to others
* Unfair delegation of duties and responsibilities
* Intimidation and threats in general.
   (Bullying, intimidation, harassment in the workplace)

'Non-physical forms of bullying include a person or group of people exerting persistent psychological violence on an individual ... The focus here is on pressure persistently applied on a single individual who frequently has no peer support.' (Irish Congress of Trade Unions: *Bullying in the workplace*)

In essence, bullying is unwanted behaviour of a physical or verbal nature which unfairly discriminates, humiliates, embarrasses, or intimidates an employee, or results in an employee feeling threatened, offended or compromised in any way. It is behaviour which undermines the confidence and self-esteem of the person being bullied. It may be perpetrated by any level of staff, i.e. manager, supervisor, or colleague.

A worker may be selected by a manager or colleague to be bullied because of a particular personality trait, or due to some perceived *difference*, such as age, race, nationality, ethnic origin, religious persuasion, political preference, membership or non-membership of a trade union, disability, or some physical characteristic. A worker may also be bullied because he or she is viewed as being weaker than the bully, or is perceived as being a threat by the bully.

In the case of persistent non-physical forms of bullying, it can often be very difficult for the victim to accumulate tangible evidence due to the covert and insidious nature of such behaviour. Attempts to ignore bullying, or a pretence at acquiescence, may encourage bullies to believe that their behaviour is harmless fun. Much bullying takes the form of picking on a single individual by making them the butt of remarks and/or aggressive behaviour. Often the victim feels totally isolated and unable to turn to anyone, either the union or management, for help.

Violence

The ICTU states that: 'Violent behaviour towards another is the most obvious form of bullying. It can take the form of assaults or deliberate pushing or jostling of an individual. Other physical forms of bullying can include persons damaging or interfering with the property of others.' (Irish Congress of Trade Unions: *Bullying in the workplace*)

Violence can be perpetrated on workers by colleagues, superiors, or members of the public. According to the Health and Safety Authority: 'Violence at work occurs where persons are verbally abused, threatened or assaulted in circumstances relating to their work.' *(Violence at work)*

Violence has also been defined as 'incidents where persons are abused, threatened, or assaulted in circumstances related to their work, involving an explicit or implicit challenge to their safety, well-being or health.' (Wynne: *Guidelines on the prevention of violence at work*, 1995)

Stress
Behaviour which seeks to coerce a worker into complying with unreasonable requests, or into remaining silent when work conditions are causing undue stress, may also be termed bullying. A useful definition of stress is: 'Stress occurs when the demands on people exceed their capacity to meet them.' (Wynne: *The experience of stress among Irish nurses*, 1993)

The Health and Safety Authority *(Workplace stress: Cause, effects and control)*, lists the following factors as potential causes of excessive stress levels at work:
* Poorly organised shiftwork
* Faulty work organisation
* Changes at work
* Poor working relationships
* Poor communication at work
* Lack of personal control over the work
* Ill-defined work roles
* Machine paced work
* Dull repetitive work
* Highly demanding tasks
* Dealing directly with the public
* The threat of violence.

Employees who are ordered to work in an environment where adequate controls on stress levels are not implemented, are routinely exposed to potential mental health risks. They are often coerced, by threats or manipulation, into carrying out their duties under highly stressful conditions. Unreasonable objectives or deadlines which are impossible to meet may be set by an organisation, causing workers to feel anxious, frustrated, and powerless.

Under Section 6 of the Safety, Health and Welfare at Work Act 1989, an employer has a duty of care to ensure the health, safety and welfare at work of all employees. Therefore, non-physical forms of bullying, violence or excessive levels of stress, as suffered by employees, may be proved unlawful under this act, and the employer be liable to pay compensation.

Pending Legislation: Employment Equality Bill
The Employment Equality Bill 1997, was published in December 1997 and is expected to be passed in the summer of 1998. Under section 23 of the bill, sexual harassment is defined for the first

time in Irish law. It outlaws sexual harassment in the workplace and in the course of employment, whether by an employer, another employee or by clients, customers, or business contacts. Sexual harassment is defined 'to include sexually offensive, humiliating or intimidating actions involving acts of physical intimacy, spoken words, gestures, or the production, display or circulation of written material or pictures, or requests for sexual favours.'

Harassment in the workplace is also defined and outlawed under section 32 of this bill. Harassment is defined as 'any act or conduct which is offensive, humiliating or intimidating on a discriminatory ground including acts of physical intimacy, spoken words, gestures, or the production, display or circulation of written material or pictures.'

Discrimination is outlawed on nine distinct grounds: 'gender, marital status, family status, sexual orientation, religious belief, age, disability, race, and membership of the travelling community.' Therefore, in the workplace it will be an offence to harass a person, or to treat anyone less favourably, on any of these grounds.

CHAPTER TWO

The extent of harassment in the workplace

So how frequently do cases of sexual harassment and bullying actually occur in the Irish workplace? As part of the research and writing of this book, I have spoken to a large cross-section of workers, employed in such diverse fields as education, health, finance, industry, technology, the military, various trades, services, and professions. I had some awareness of the extent of harassment before embarking on this book, but I was quite overwhelmed by the sheer number of people who I spoke with who had either experienced harassment at work themselves, or who had stories to tell about work-mates, family or friends who had been victimised at work in Ireland.

It was very common for those who had experienced harassment to feel a great deal of embarrassment when talking about their experiences. None of those I spoke with had brought a case to the labour court. Very few people had received any form of compensation for harassment from an employer. Several people had raised the matter with their trade union. The majority had never reported the harassment, but had bided their time, until an opportunity for new employment presented itself.

Irish Statistics

Sexual Harassment

At present, there are no reliable statistics on the occurrence of sexual harassment in the workplace in Ireland. Official cases taken by Irish workers against employers are minuscule.

According to The Labour Court's Annual Report (1996), two cases involving alleged sexual harassment were referred to the labour court, under Section 27 of the Employment Equality Act (1977). Both cases were processed and successfully won by the employees during the year. Claimants were awarded damages of £2,000 and £3,200 respectively. One other case of alleged sexual harassment was settled by the parties during the labour court investigations.

The Employment Equality Agency (EEA) receives many enquiries each year on the issue of sexual harassment (see table below).

Enquiries Re Sexual Harassment to Employment Equality Agency
(Source: EEA Annual Reports: 1993 to 1996)

Year	No of Enquiries
1993	190
1994	307
1995	267
1996	173

The EEA reports that the decline in enquiries over the last two years coincided with the introduction of their code of practice in 1994. This encouraged employers to issue a policy on sexual harassment to all staff, which may have reduced the need for employees to contact EEA.

In 1993 a Landsdowne Market Research Survey was commissioned by *The Sunday Press* into the occurrence of sexual harassment of women in the workplace. The results below show the percentage of women surveyed who said they had experienced various forms of sexual harassment. Between 7% and 14% of respondents admitted to having been subjected to the types of harassment indicated. What is most striking is the percentage of women who were ill-informed as to what constituted sexual harassment. For example, 37% of women did not think that 'unwanted demand for sex or dates' was sexual harassment.

The Sunday Press survey into sexual harassment
of women in the Workplace

Behaviour experienced by women	% of women who experienced this type of harassment	% of women who considered behaviour to be sexual harassment
Touched/brushed against	14	63
Unwanted demand for sex or dates	7	63
Grabbed	7	54
Stared at/Leered at by men	11	28
Exposed to pin-ups	7	17
Told sexual jokes/re-	12	16

In Northern Ireland, a survey on attitudes to work, conducted with the assistance of the European Commission in 1986, found that 22% of women reported sexual harassment, with 45% of these saying that it occurred often. (*Equal Opportunities for Northern Ireland*, 1993)

Bullying
According to IBEC, bullying arises in all facets of life, and due to the hierarchical structure of most work places, very few employees are likely to go through their working lives without experiencing some degree of bullying. (*Workplace bullying: A variation of harassment*, 1996, p. 1)

The Irish Congress of Trade Unions (ICTU) states that it is difficult to establish the full extent of bullying at work because precise figures do not exist. However, the recent experience of unions, both in Ireland and abroad, suggest that bullying in the workplace is more prevalent than the numbers who complained in the past would indicate. The Congress Information Service has recently experienced an increase in the number of queries and complaints about bullying at work. This increase, according to ICTU, is likely to be due to workers' increased awareness as a result of media publicity since the latter part of 1995.

Unions have encouraged workers to speak out and to seek help for many years, and have been effectively helping victims of bullying who have come forward. According to ICTU, the full extent of the problem will not be known until a work environment is created which will ensure that no worker who is being bullied or harassed will have to suffer in silence.

An MSF (Manufacturing Science Finance Union) survey of workplace representatives in Britain and Ireland in 1994 showed 30% of respondents thought that bullying was a significant problem in the workplace. 72% of respondents said their employer had no policy for dealing with bullying. MSF identified types of organisations where bullying was most prevalent. This included firms where workers had high workloads, where a macho competitive culture existed, where there is rapid change and uncertainty, and where personnel management is poorly developed and rudimentary.

The Irish Nursing Organisation (INO) conducted a study in 1997 as to the extent of bullying in nursing. The following facts were revealed:

* More than 9 in 10 nurses stated they had been victims of bullying
* 3 in 10 were bullied by nurses of the same grade, and 23% said a member of the medical team was their harasser. Other bullies included ward sisters, theatre sisters, unit nursing officers, assistant matrons, and directors of nursing
* 79% of bullying occurred in hospitals, 16% in community care, 2% in the nursing care sector, and 1% by GPs in surgeries
* Approximately 3% were subjected to threatening behaviour although actual assaults also took place
* The most common form of bullying (87%) was verbal, with an identical number reporting psychological bullying.

Violence

In 1993, the Health and Safety Authority stated that 4% of all reported workplace accidents in the Irish workplace were due to violence. The sectors mostly involved were health and social workers, public administration, community and personal services, mining and quarrying, transport and communications. (*Violence at work*)

The INO commissioned the Work Research Center to conduct a survey into the amount of stress experienced by Irish nurses in 1993. The report produced some very disturbing results as to the incidence of assault on nurses. 39.3% of the sample reported experiencing assault from patients at some time in their career, with 5% reporting assault from visitors. Small percentages also reported assault from intruders, fellow nurses and colleagues, giving an overall figure of 46.6% of the sample who had been assaulted in the course of their nursing career.

A recent survey of general practitioners, undertaken in Dublin, found that 44.4% of male doctors and 32.5% of female doctors suffered from some form of aggression or assault in the previous year. Over 40% of doctors had had their cars or surgeries damaged, and some had even had their surgeries burnt to the ground. (O'Connell: 1994)

The National Bus and Rail Union reported that there had been at least one violent attack on Dublin Bus staff on each day in the previous month and that at present more than 70 drivers are on long-term sick-leave because of attacks on bus workers. (*The Irish Times*, May 1995)

Stress

The INO 1993 survey into the amount of stress experienced by Irish nurses revealed that high stress levels were reported by 60.9% of nurses (due to too many nursing tasks), 57% (not enough time to provide emotional support to patients), 48% (lack of involvement in policy/decision making), and 46.8% (lack of consultation/communications).

BRITISH STATISTICS

Sexual Harassment

In the United Kingdom, a Labour Research Department survey of workplace unions, branches and women representatives, found 73% of those surveyed had reported some form of sexual harassment had taken place at work. (*Sexual harassment at work – Guidance on prevention*, 1993)

Research into sexual harassment conducted by the Industrial Society in the UK produced the following findings:

* Nine out of ten of those harassed were female
* The most common form of sexual harassment is verbal, e.g. comments about clothing, looks, etc.
* Three out of four of those harassed report a negative impact on their work situation: increased absenteeism, inability to work with colleagues, being under severe stress, etc.
* Only 5% of those harassed filed a formal complaint. More than 70% of those who did file a complaint or who referred a case to the tribunal, reported an improvement in their situation.

(*The law on sexual harassment*, IBEC) REF

A recent British survey into the treatment of female secretaries by their male bosses revealed that:

* Half of secretaries are subjected to sexism in the workplace
* 15% say they had been sexually propositioned by their bosses, who had invited them to have sex or asked them to perform some kind of sex act
* More than half of the women surveyed said they were expected to make their boss coffee, and buy his lunch
* 18% said their boss expected them to buy presents for their wives, mistresses and children
* 14% said their boss had given them clothes to mend.

(*The Evening Herald*, 16 March 1998: 'Sexism still being employed') REF

Bullying

In Britain, the Institute of Personnel and Development (IPD) carried out a major survey of 1,000 workers into bullying, over a five year period. In 1996, when the survey was concluded, it was found that:

* One in eight workers were victims of bullying
* The majority of bullying was perpetrated by senior staff: almost one-third of victims said that the bully was the head of the department or section, and 16% pointed the finger at the chief executive or managing director
* Bullying behaviour consisted of unfair and excessive criticism, publicly insulting the victim, ignoring their point of view and constantly changing or setting unrealistic work targets, constant under-valuation of their efforts at work, shouting and abusive behaviour. Actual physical assault was reported by 8% of victims
* Over half of those who had experienced bullying said it was commonplace in their organisation
* Nearly three-quarters (72%) of victims of bullying said they had suffered from work-related stress in the last five years
* One third of victims did not raise the problem with anyone at work.

Staffordshire University, on behalf of the BBC, carried out a survey in 1994 into bullying at work. The findings were that 78% of 1137 men and women sampled had witnessed bullying in the workplace, while 51% had experienced it themselves. 68% of these had been bullied before the age of 25. Most had been bullied by managers: 41% by line managers and 30% by senior managers.

In a second survey of 53 of Britain's top 100 companies, commissioned by the BBC, 75% of employees acknowledged the potential for bullying to occur, yet there were no formal policies in place to deal with bullying. (*Bullying at work*, BBC)

Violence

The UK home office reported an increase of 3% in both 1990 and 1991, and of 6% in 1992, in the number of workplace related violent incidents. (Home Office Statistical Bulletin, 1992)

In the UK the number of criminal attacks on banks has increased rapidly in recent years, from 868 in 1989 to 1633 in 1991. (Wahl, 1994) The Building Societies Association in the UK also reported an increase in robberies from 368 in 1988 to 940 in 1992. (Reynolds)

A major retail group (Beck and Willis, 1991) reported that 300 incidents of actual or threatened violence had occurred in a six-month period in a survey of 1032 stores in 1989.

Stress

Figures obtained from the Department of Employment show that stress caused or exacerbated by work emerged as the second largest category of occupational disease in the UK. There are an estimated 182,000 cases each year in England and Wales alone. (*Bullying at work*, BBC)

EUROPEAN STATISTICS

A report published by the European Foundation for the Improvement of Living and Working Conditions in 1997 stated that over 13 million people are subjected to violence or intimidation in the workplace throughout the European union. There are 147 million people at work in the 15 member states of the EU, and of these 83% are employees. For this report, more than 1,000 employees were interviewed in each state by the foundation. More than 9% of workers claim to have been subjected to violence or intimidation in the workplace. The report estimates that 3 million employees are subjected to sexual harassment, 6 million to physical violence, and 12 million to psychological violence through bullying and abuse. The report says that definitions of violence may vary from country to country, and from occupation to occupation, but that violence of one kind or another is clearly a major problem, and one which will need to be monitored very closely in future.

Research across the European Union and in each member state reveals varying degrees of sexual abuse at work. One Spanish survey found 84% of women questioned had experienced some form of sexual harassment. In Germany, 72% of women said they had been sexually harassed at work. (*Sexual harassment at work – Guidance on prevention*, 1993) The report of the European Commission (1987) reported the following percentages of women surveyed who said they had experienced sexual harassment at work: Spain 84%, Germany 59%, The Netherlands 58%, Great Britain 51%, Italy 47.8%, Belgium 30%, and Northern Ireland 22%. (*Report of EC Seminar: Sexual harassment at work*, 1991)

The above figures give us some indication of the extent of harassment experienced by Irish, British and European workers.

SIPTU: Interview with Frank O'Malley, Branch Secretary

So what has SIPTU, the largest union in the country, representing some 200,000 Irish workers, to say about the extent of harassment in the workplace? Frank O'Malley has over twenty-seven years of union experience, working in such areas as aviation, insurance and finance. He is currently SIPTU Branch Secretary of the Hotels, Restaurants and Catering Division in Liberty Hall, Dublin, serving over 5,000 members.

'In my experience bullying is multi-faceted, and permeates all levels and sectors of employment. It is a huge problem, which unions have been aware of for decades. It is only recently beginning to surface, however, in terms of national awareness. Sexual harassment is also widely prevalent, but is much easier to define. There are so many behaviours which may constitute bullying. We are all familiar with the classic type of bullying – the inflicting of physical or mental violence. But we need to extend this basic definition. For example, is it bullying if you're working in an organisation which is not open, and where promotion is only available to a certain type of person – Irish, male, non-union, and aged between 30 and 40? Or is it bullying where an employee is brought under extreme pressure to meet company targets, which necessitates working a sixty-hour week, and still the unreasonable objectives can't be met?

Unions have no problem with firms who seek to maximise productivity, as long as the objectives are realistic and are agreed with the union. When impossible targets are set by an organisation, this puts terrible pressure on staff who are expected to meet them. This is especially true in the area of sales. Let's take, for example, the case of a salesman who has reached the company objective in the proceeding year. He has broken his back this year, it has been a bumper year in terms of commission, but he knows it'll be impossible to maintain this level of sales in the coming year. Competition is too great from new firms in the area, and he'll count himself lucky if he can retain his current number of clients. He's called in by his boss, complimented on his success, and then informed that next year he's expected to do even better. He's told the board of directors want to see an increase in sales next year of 15%. He tells his boss it's not feasible, given the current climate. He's told in no uncertain terms that he's got no choice, he has to meet the required objectives. But how is he to motivate himself to sell more when he knows it's impossible? That kind of pressure is soul-destroying. It's yet another facet of workplace bullying.

The real problem is that bullying is so hard to define, and subsequently to prove. It hasn't been possible to compile official figures as to numbers of workers who have been bullied or sexually harassed, not only due to a problem with definition, but also because of the reticence of victims in coming forward, and in seeking help. That situation is now changing, and in SIPTU we're seeing a mushrooming of complaints of bullying being made by our members. Cases of sexual harassment against women are not as prevalent as they once were, but the psychological abuse of women seems to be increasing.

I know of employers who are unreasonable bullies. I know of firms who deliberately employ people who have broken relationships, just because these people are more vulnerable and can be easily exploited. I've also encountered workplaces where the employer expects his staff to give him sexual favours in return for promotion and salary increases. These are examples of pure greed and show an abominable abuse of power. Bullies usually prey on the most weak and vulnerable sectors of the workforce, those who are least likely to stand up and make a complaint. Some bullies can be so devious and smart, making life a misery for a worker who has joined a union, doing everything to force him or her out, but all under the guise of monitoring job performance. Bullies often try to reinforce a person's lack of confidence by constant criticism and abuse. Their desired objective may be to force the person out, to get someone in such a state of ill-health that he'll have to leave. This type of bullying is insidious, pernicious and emotionally crippling to the individual concerned

Workers who are being persistently bullied need support from, and representation by, unions. Some employers, however, have a dread of unions. This boils down to their fear of increased costs if a union gets a foothold. This fear in my experience is misguided, rather like being penny wise and pounds foolish. In the long-term employers save money when workers join a union. The whole business sharpens up and runs more efficiently. Everything is done above board, tax and PRSI are deducted, every employee is handed a payslip and is paid on time. Definite job descriptions are drawn up which attracts more highly skilled and trained staff. Customer service is greatly improved as you no longer have a situation where one waiter is left to deal with thirty people, or where a manager is left with insufficient staff at the busiest period of the week.

The introduction of unions into a firm puts a whole structure in place which is advantageous to both workers and employers. This insures that policies and procedures for dealing with bullying and harassment are agreed and implemented, and that staff-management disputes are more effectively dealt with. Employers who set up businesses to make a quick buck aren't concerned with staff welfare, but those who really want to make a success of their business will benefit from union intervention. I know of hotels which can't get skilled staff because their reputation is so poor. When workers see that employers are involved in co-operative agreements with unions, then they're more inclined to seek employment, and to stay there, as it seems an attractive move, career-wise.

What unions want to achieve is a working environment where all members of staff are equally respected, valued, and given sufficient remuneration for their work and service. Such a staff is an asset to any organisation. When workers are happy with their treatment and conditions they are more likely to be friendly and attentive to customers, which will further accentuate the firm's growth.

The presence of unions in a workplace can go a long way to eradicating bullying and harassment. Unions insure that agreed policies on bullying and harassment are drawn up with management, and issued to every member of staff. At least if staff are made aware of what constitutes bullying and sexual harassment, and are informed that a structure is in place to deal with complaints in a fair and confidential manner, then victims are more likely to come forward and confront their tormentor. Likewise, when bullies are made aware of the consequences of their behaviour, and the commitment of the firm to an harassment-free workplace, they are much less likely to persist with an abusive or vindictive campaign. '

CHAPTER THREE

Causes of harassment at work

AT ORGANISATIONAL LEVEL

Prevailing ethos of organisation is one of boss management
Boss management is based on the premise that workers can be coerced into doing specified tasks by the promise of reward or by the threat of punishment. There is no attempt made to satisfy workers' basic psychological needs, such as their social and self-esteem needs. This creates a workplace where staff are divided into two categories: those who are rewarded for their blind obedience and loyalty, and those who are forced to conform by the threat of punishment.

In reality, however, workers resent being told what to do without being involved, consulted, or treated as an important part of the organisation. They may perform allotted tasks out of fear, or to get some reward, but they will never aim for quality work, nor draw on their real potential for creativity and excellence.

Workers are kept under control by the enforcement of a long list of rules and regulations, breach of which will most likely result in disciplinary action. Workers may feel actively discouraged from airing their grievances, or obtaining impartial representation, as disagreement with management or company policy is viewed as highly undesirable. Sexism, racism, and favouritism are the norm in such a workplace. Since workers' social needs are ignored, this leads to low staff morale and a general state of discontent.

A high degree of conformity is expected in a boss-managed firm. Individuality, creativity and personal flair are looked on with suspicion. Workers are promoted, not on traits such as strong leadership skills, good communication skills or organisational ability, but based on the extent of their obedience to management. Therefore it is often the case that, psychologically, the weakest and most pliable workers are chosen to be promoted to managerial positions.

The boss manager is quite typical of the theory X manager portrayed by Donald McGregor. McGregor devised two management styles which were basically sets of assumptions about workers' behaviour. Theory X regards workers as being lazy and irresponsible, requiring control and coercion. Theory Y views workers as liking work. These workers have no need for coercion, are committed to contributing towards the organisation's goals, seek responsibility, and are creative and industrious at work. McGregor's concept has been helpful in identifying extreme types of management styles.

Misuse and Abuse of Power
So what is power? Does power mean control? Does power mean responsibility? In essence, power in the workplace involves making decisions. The ultimate decision will be made by the person who has the most power. Some organisations, like the boss-managers above, are built on fear: 'If I allow workers to have an input into decisions, even those which effect their own working lives, they'll take over. So we'll just have to keep them subdued and powerless!' Other firms recognise the value of their workers' skills and experience, and encourage open discussion and collaboration among staff before decisions are made.

And what of personal power? In a democracy we like to feel we have the power to live the kind of life we choose. Yet most of us have experienced times in our lives when we felt powerless. As children, many of us encountered adults who took away our power, who made us feel small and insignificant. As adults, there are those who have never regained their sense of personal power. Perhaps they have grown used to giving away power to those in authority. Then there are those who habitually abuse power. Often these men and women were themselves victims of abuse as children. Many abusers of power feel a basic insecurity and anger, which they try to disguise by humiliating others and by momentarily boosting their own egos.

In the work environment, the way in which power is distributed and used among the workforce is of paramount importance to the success of the organisation, and to the welfare of its workers. By virtue of the hierarchical nature of most Irish workplaces, power is rarely equally distributed among staff. In a psychologically unhealthy workplace, power is routinely misused and abused. There are organisations which actually promote bullying as a 'style' of management. Newly appointed managers are then inculcated into this bullying work culture. Their 'training' comes from observing other managers coercing workers into carrying out allotted tasks, and then screaming at them or criticising them abusively if the job is not done to their satisfaction. Having the power to bully can be seen as a perk of management in such an organisation.

Two types of managers who misuse and abuse their power are typically encountered in the boss-managed workplace. These are the dictator, and the incompetent manager. The bully is also frequently encountered where boss-management prevails, whether as a formally appointed manager or supervisor, or as a worker who assumes informal power due to the favouritism or moral weakness of those in authority. The sexual harasser is also more likely to be active in such a dysfunctional workplace.

The dictator

The dictator is supremely arrogant, egocentric, and begrudges every penny that the firm has to spend on employing staff. Most typically the dictator owns the firm or is given carte-blanche by a board of directors to run the show. Workers must know their place, and must not displease their boss in any way. This type of boss is always driven by a huge need for power. He or she is basically a bully, and uses threats, manipulation, and coercion to force others to conform to his or her will. The dictator cannot tolerate any degree of criticism, and so surrounds him or herself with weak, frightened subordinates.

This type of boss is often emotionally unbalanced, prone to temper tantrums and outbursts of ferocious anger. The worker is seen as not much more than a slave, whose function is to complete tasks on time so as to increase the firm's profits. The organisation is usually 'closed' to the outside world – unions are outlawed, psychological research is scorned, and legislation to improve workers' rights is only begrudgingly introduced. The worker's welfare is irrelevant, though steps will be taken to insure that minimum conditions are met, to keep adverse publicity at bay.

The dictator sets the tone for the entire organisation. Even the most enthusiastic lead manager will soon become disillusioned and deeply frustrated working under such a boss, due to the lack of communication, support, mentoring, delegating and training, and the general atmosphere of negativity which prevails. To 'get on' in such a workplace, a 'loyal' worker must set all personal values aside, give absolute allegiance to the boss, and perform any nasty tasks assigned, such as spying on co-workers or giving those who fall foul of the Fuhrer a hard time. High levels of staff turnover and absenteeism are the norm in such a dysfunctional environment where workers at all levels feel highly stressed, frightened, and frequently out of control.

Case Study: Mary, twenty-six-year-old wages clerk

Mary had worked in a large insurance company in Dublin before being appointed by a leading car sales firm. The first thing which struck her as strange was when she said 'good morning' to the managing director; he stared right through her and quickly walked past, without uttering a word. It didn't take her long to discover that everyone in the organisation was terrified of him. He had a habit of making life a misery for those he took a personal dislike to. He told one girl that he didn't like the look of her and the following month her contract was discontinued.

Mary had only been there a week when an angry scene broke out between her own boss and the MD. Mary had never heard anything like the cursing and swearing which came from her boss's office. She felt embarrassed, as it was her own boss who was being pulled asunder, in front of his workers. That afternoon her boss called her in and chastised her for making a mistake. He said he wouldn't tolerate this kind of messy work. She was greatly taken aback, and tried to explain that it would take her a few weeks to settle in. 'Never talk back like that to me!' he screamed. 'I won't take that kind of lip from the likes of you!' Mary had never been treated like this. She felt hurt and angry. She figured it was his way of trying not to lose face in front of his workers after what had happened that morning. Then abruptly he said, 'Get back to your work.'

Mary witnessed many similar scenes over the six months she spent there. She described it as the worst time of her life. She had never seen such a turnover of staff, as many people weren't prepared to put up with such abusive treatment, not to mention the appalling wages. She had asked her colleagues about joining a union but they looked really scared when she mentioned it. They told her in no uncertain terms that the MD would go absolutely berserk if anyone joined a union. He was a very powerful man, she was told, with friends in high places, and resources to the world's end. She was also warned not to mention it to anyone else, as the MD had his spies constantly on the look-out for trouble-makers.

The degrading scenes occurred regularly. At least once a week some unfortunate person would be demeaned by either the MD, or by her angry and hostile boss. On one occasion her boss humiliated her in front of the whole department for some alleged mistake. Mary had had enough. She decided to seek alternative employment where she could earn a living without having to endure and witness such persistent bullying and abuse.

The incompetent manager

This type of manager is basically very insecure and feels quite inadequate. He or she has problems relating well to peers, and hence has very poor people skills. Promotion to management will usually have arisen as a result of technical or other specialist abilities, in an organisation where there is little awareness of the importance of establishing good worker-management relations, or in management training. The incompetent manager simply does not manage his or her staff. For a period, a situation may develop where workers do as they please, aware that their manager cannot assume any degree of authority, nor motivate staff in any way. This type of manager may initially try to be accepted as 'one of the workers'. Ultimately this approach will fail as problems occur in the workplace, and the manager refuses to accept responsibility for the needs and welfare of staff. The manager will never push for better conditions for workers, or represent an individual case to higher management, but will avoid confrontation at all costs.

Workers under such a manager may find themselves virtually leaderless. Any initiative which workers take in establishing more effective work procedures will usually be seen as a threat by their insecure manager. Frustration and apathy is a natural progression for workers who are issued with no policy, who are given no incentive to produce quality work, and who are completely unmotivated. The incompetent manager may then delegate the management role to a subordinate, with whom there is a particular affinity.

In such an atmosphere, cliques and favouritism are rife. To feel more secure, the incompetent manager will often make promotions based on personal preferences rather than on ability. This can create a serious division and deep resentment between staff. Some workers may find themselves completely isolated, and even ignored, by such a manager. If workers try to address this situation constructively, any such attempts at communication are likely to be construed as personal criticism by the manager, and workers may be further alienated. A complete breakdown in communication may occur between this type of manager and some of the stronger members of staff. This will only fuel workers' feelings of frustration and apathy, and a state of rebellion, bordering on sabotage, can easily ensue. At this stage the manager may hand these 'troublesome' workers over to a superior, or to personnel, to be disciplined, demoted, or dismissed for their disruptive influence on the workplace.

Case Study: Jack, thirty-two-year-old purchasing clerk

'I had worked in many different companies, before joining X & Co. Ltd, a manufacturing firm. Immediately I knew there was a problem with the manager. He was very friendly with two female staff members. They'd get together during working hours and trade blue jokes, which I found to be very distracting. Once I entered his office to find him with his arm around one of his favourites. This type of unprofessional conduct certainly did little to win my respect for his position as manager. I also noticed that when he'd walk into the general office area, and neither of his favourites were there, he'd turn around and leave without saying a word. He seemed to have a particular problem relating to men, and when I had reason to talk to him alone he seemed nervous and unsure of himself.

I often heard him laughing about the chief executive with his two favourites, and saying derogatory things about other managers and staff. There were several guys who got a terrible going over from him, but always behind their backs. One guy had a speech impediment, so he was an easy target to ridicule. Another guy had a strong rural accent and was the daily butt of vicious mimicry. Then there was a lad who had a slight limp, so that was more fuel for his pathetic jokes. There was one girl he never spoke to and actively tried to remove from the department. I'm sure he felt threatened by her because she was studying management outside of work. It was all quite sick, and very distasteful.

I discussed his behaviour with several other workers who had been there when he was first appointed. They said that initially he'd been so nervous that his hands shook when he spoke

to a group of two or three people. He'd given the impression
that he was going to stand back and allow the workers to manage themselves. He'd said on several occasions that he didn't
care what the workers did, just as long as the work was done
and there were no complaints from other managers. So everyone more or less did as they pleased and there was a general
state of chaos. There was no motivation whatsoever to do anything but the bare minimum. Worse still there was no communication: he wouldn't talk to anyone except the two females, and
as a result of this there was a complete split in the department.
Some of the lads had approached him previously to arrange a
meeting to discuss their grievances, but they could never pin
him down. There was a formal grievance procedure in the firm
but no one had any faith in it. It was the common opinion of
workers that personnel always came down on the side of management.

I soon began to understand their frustration. I took the initiative to establish a new, more efficient, invoicing system. I sent
my manager the proposal but he never even mentioned it. In
fact, I felt he positively avoided me, staring at the floor when I
met him in the corridor. When I was there three months he finally
called a meeting, but only to inform us that his two 'favourites'
were being promoted to supervisor. These people had no training and no suitable experience, as far as I could see. A near
mutiny ensued. The workers went on a go-slow. Personnel were
finally called in to take control, and several workers were
moved to other departments. Nothing was ever said to the manager, who was most definitely the cause of the whole fiasco. As
far as I know he's still there today. I left about two months later.'

The Bully

In a boss-managed organisation, bullies can run riot, whether as
managers or workers. Since the psychological welfare of workers is not a priority, there is very little protection for workers
who fall foul of the classic bully. A bully is someone who uses
strength or power to coerce, persecute, or oppress others by
using force or threats. The psychological profile of the bully is
very similar to that of the dictator: emotionally immature and
unstable, power-hungry, with little or no respect for fellow
workers.

Basically bullies are very insecure people, no matter how
competent they may appear. They like to feel powerful by humil-

iating a particular individual in front of others. Almost certainly they were subject to constant criticism or humiliation themselves as children, and were repeatedly blamed for things that went wrong which they had no control over. Once in a position of power, these individuals use aggressive and oppressive behaviours to force workers into conforming to their wishes. Their moods tend to be unpredictable and potentially explosive. Bullies frequently shout, scream, rip up reports, use obscene language, and behave like spoiled children, throwing a tantrum when they feel angry or frustrated. Threats, abuse, sexism, racism, and the isolation and ridicule of selected workers may all occur at the hands of an unchecked bully.

This type of person is often quite cowardly if confronted by a strong manager, but will reign supreme if allowed to form cliques, and to assume power over other workers. Since there is little or no management training in a boss-managed organisation, nor any awareness of the psychological effects on workers of such threatening and intimidating behaviour, workers faced with a bully in their workplace can feel overwhelmed and powerless.

Although many bullies are overtly aggressive, a bully may also torment and harass an employee in a very insidious or manipulative manner. It may be very difficult for the victim to obtain tangible proof. An example of this is where a bullying manager adopts a strategy to discommode a worker by heaping on excessive volumes of work, or demanding that work be completed in unreasonable deadlines. Thus, it may appear to higher levels of management that there is a work performance problem with this particular worker. Likewise, a bully may constantly monitor a worker's conduct, scrutinising lists of telephone calls and time-keeping records. Since no one is infallible, whenever the worker comes in late or makes an extra-long telephone call, the bully can report a problem with this worker's conduct.

Bullies may also have psychopathic tendencies. These people fail to accept responsibility for their actions, or the effects which their behaviour has on others. They may feel no one has the right to criticise, question, challenge or contradict their opinion or their way of doing things. These bullies may have been spoiled or made to feel 'special' as children, and may believe that they are the centre of the universe.

In general, bullies tend to:
    * Always need to be in control

* Blame everyone else but themselves
* Make life difficult for those they dislike
* Refuse to delegate because they believe no one else can be trusted
* Feel insecure and inadequate
* Never admit they are wrong
* Have poor communication skills
* Feel under stress themselves
* Set tasks which they know are unreasonable or are beyond the person's current capabilities
* Refuse reasonable requests
* Take credit for other people's work
* Be vindictive, tyrannical, devious and/or dishonest
* Appear charming to outsiders and superiors
* Be unbalanced emotionally, and prone to bouts of ferocious anger.

In a survey carried out by the National Association of School-masters and Union of Women Teachers (NASUWT) in the UK and Northern Ireland (1997), into the incidence of bullying perpetrated against teachers, it was found that 59% of bullies were male, 55% were aged in their forties, and 52% were head-teachers. Victims were most likely to be female (64%), in their forties (40%), and at the standard scale of teaching (40%). The report identified ten different types of bullies:

* Unfocused exploder – blows up if anyone gets in the way when angry
* Focused exploder – shouts at weak members of staff
* Personal dislikes – targets certain staff
* Threat responder – bullies those who might pose a threat
* Anger parcel passer – being bullied by superior, so bullies subordinates
* Deliberate bully – gives staff a hard time. Believes it's the best way to get good work done
* Exasperated bully – has tried to be nice in the past. Has been disappointed with results, so now is angry and frustrated.
* Sadistic bully – simply derives pleasure from bullying others
* Resignation seeker – makes life hell for anyone they want to force into resigning
* Macho image seeker – bullies to bolster their own ego.

Constant criticism, destructive innuendo and sarcasm were the most prevalent forms of bullying (57%). The most common effects on victims were: loss of confidence (74%), dread going to work (57%), and sleepless nights (56%).

The profile of the victim
Bullies select victims for one of two reasons. Either the person is too conscientious and successful at his or her job, and the bully feels threatened and jealous, or the person is in some way vulnerable and an easy target for insults, ridicule, threats or persistent criticism. A more detailed profile of either type of victim is given below:

Conscientious victim:
* High achiever at work
* Efficient, organised, and diligent
* Highly intelligent and knowledgeable
* Confident, out-spoken, and possessing superior social skills
* Higher qualifications
* Over-enthusiastic about work
* Popular among colleagues or customers
* Attractive and youthful
* Creative, with natural flair.

Vulnerable victim:
* Different from most staff members with regard to age, marital status, social background, sexual orientation, or physical characteristics, including disability
* Vulnerable due to recent bereavement, break-up of relationship, maternity leave, prolonged sickness
* Poor social skills, timidity and shyness.

A study done by Maarit Vartia (1996) into the reasons for bullying as perceived by a group of Finnish municipal employees, showed the following results:
* Envy – 63%
* Weak superior – 38%
* Competition for tasks or advancements – 38%
* Competition for the superior's favour and approval – 34%
* Insecurity (risk of losing job) – 23%
* Age (oldest/youngest) – 22%
* Being different from others – 21%
* Unsatisfactory and monotonous work – 7%.

Warning signs of being bullied/intimidated:

* Problems begin when a new manager or co-worker is appointed
* Constant petty criticisms are made about your work, although in the past your reviews were satisfactory, and your work was rarely criticised
* Challenging, interesting and responsible work is withdrawn from you without good reason
* You are told to carry out a task for which you were not employed, and which is beneath your grade
* A boss or colleague deliberately sabotages or impedes your work performance
* Work is withheld from you, or incorrect information is deliberately supplied
* Work targets or guidelines are constantly changed, making it impossible to reach them
* Over-monitoring of your work occurs, with malicious intent
* You are told to comply with a new rule which is demeaning or discriminatory in nature
* Your manager tends to take credit for your ideas, so that you feel annoyed and frustrated, and your creativity becomes stifled
* Your work load is increased, and your deadlines are reduced to an impossible level, so that you are in effect set-up for certain failure
* Applications for leave, training and promotion are blocked
* You are demoted for no justifiable reason
* Your boss instigates complaints from colleagues or customers, to make it appear that you are unreliable or incompetent
* You are no longer invited to business meetings or social events which you once regularly attended
* Your efforts at work are constantly undervalued
* You are criticised for making mistakes, when this is untrue or exaggerated
* You are discouraged or actively hindered from airing grievances
* Your telephone calls are listened to, your personal correspondence is opened, your personal belongings are searched, or your visits to the toilet are monitored
* Your manager flies into temper tantrums, shouts, uses abusive language, and loses emotional control at the least provocation

* Personal comments, insults and name-calling are used by your boss or colleagues to demean, humiliate and control
* Malicious rumours and gossip which are unfounded, concerning certain staff members, are spread around the workplace
* Certain employees are persecuted through physical assault or threats which instills fear
* You are constantly stared at, spied upon, and your movements scrutinised
* You are moved to a smaller office, or to the corner of an office, without reasonable grounds
* You receive accusatory memos for breaking petty rules, whereas other staff members who behave in exactly the same way receive no such reprimand
* A clique develops in your section, from which you are isolated, and your manager either ignores this, or shows favouritism to members of the clique
* You feel powerless, alienated, and dread coming to work each morning.

Case Study: Robert, forty-two-year-old telecommunications engineer
'I had worked for the same semi-state body for three years. I was on friendly terms with most of the staff, and I really enjoyed my work. Then Ben joined. He was also employed as an engineer and worked in the same office. He seemed to take an instant dislike to me. He had a real chip on his shoulder about me. We were poles apart. For one, I was single, and had a very moderate lifestyle, never being a subscriber to the consumer society. Ben kept on pestering me, jeering me, and speculating about all the money I must have stashed away in the bank. He was always boasting about his big car, his semi-detached house, his beautiful wife and children, and his trendy clothes and lifestyle. He'd get a real kick out of insulting me, especially when there was an audience present. He just couldn't tolerate a person who had a different approach to life than himself.

There was also a major difference in our attitudes to work. I worked diligently at my desk, because I liked my work. He would take long tea-breaks, and would often disappear early in the afternoon and woe betide anyone who would ask him where he was going! He started checking up on my every move, even writing down the time I arrived to work each morning. It was a real nuisance having him looking over my shoulder, when he had no authority whatsoever over me.

He was an out and out bully. He was a big guy, well over six feet. There were a few other guys who he also threatened and abused over the years. I witnessed him chasing one guy around the office, and twisting another guy's arm behind his back. Most of the workers were afraid of him. He started to tackle anyone who was friendly with me, trying to isolate me. He'd sneer and criticise everything about me. There was little I could do about it. He'd try to get the whole crowd on my back. On a few occasions I was beset with a barrage of abuse from all sides. He had his henchmen to do his dirty work as well. There was a clique of about ten of them who obeyed his every word. Once Ben came up behind me, and almost spat into my face, "I can do anything I like to you!"

Another habit of his was to give me a diatribe of abuse whenever I was talking to a third party, just to embarrass me, I suppose. I could never get to the root of what it was about me that obsessed him, or why he hounded me. There were things which I was sure he had done maliciously to discommode me, but I never had any proof. Like the night I found my bicycle tyres punctured, and the numerous times important items went missing from my desk. I'd also find insulting cartoons and posters, calling me names like 'scrooge', written up on the notice-board or stuck to my desk. It was a relentless and malicious campaign. At times I was very angry. A few times I felt like strangling him, just to put an end to my torment. It seemed that nothing short of murder would stop him. I developed a sudden illness during the height of his campaign, and I'm sure it was related to the stress and frustration I felt, day in and day out.

I approached his section head but that was a joke. I went to the union about him several times. I had noted down all of the abusive incidences and I gave copies of these to my union. Then there'd be a short lull in Ben's campaign against me, but before long his old abusive pattern would inevitably reinstate itself. He got on very well with his boss, who chose to ignore the bullying. There was no real machinery available for dealing with a co-worker who was a bully. A lot of other managers were even afraid of him because he was so difficult to handle. They were definitely scared to confront him. He was finally moved when part of his section was transferred to another location. It made a hell of a difference to my working life to be rid of him. He had been the bane of my working life, on a daily basis, for almost ten years.'

The sexual harasser

Like all forms of sexual abuse, sexual harassment is most often, though not exclusively, perpetrated by men against women. Unless there is a physical element to the harassment, however, many men do not consider that sexual harassment is taking place. Indeed, many men believe that sexual harassment is rare, only occurring in isolated and exceptional circumstances. Women's experiences, however, completely contradict this assumption. The problem seems to stem, on a sliding scale, from a genuine lack of awareness to the cumulative effects of sexual jokes and comments, to a complete disregard for the woman's rights as a human being.

The man who deliberately harasses a female colleague may do so for a variety of reasons. Most typically these will include the desire for power and control, and the deep-seated need to hurt or humiliate the woman. A sexual harasser is often:

* Insecure about his masculinity and sexuality. He may feel that the only way he can avoid rejection by a woman is to force her into a sexual encounter by using threats, coercion, or physical strength. Such a man is often full of self-doubt, especially if he is approaching middle age, and feels unattractive and unfulfilled.

* Hostile toward or fearful of women. A difficult childhood with a domineering mother, or a thwarted love affair, can leave a man feeling hurt, angry and frustrated. These feelings may then be turned against all women, including female colleagues and subordinates.

* Consumed by the need to dominate and manipulate others. Men who need to feel secure and powerful by dominating those who are in a weaker or more vulnerable position, may select women to sexually exploit or demean who do not pose a threat, and who are too fearful to fight back.

* Insecure about his ability at work. A man who feels unable to fairly compete and win promotion against a female 'rival' may seek to demean her and ruin her confidence by sexually harassing her. This can also occur if a manager feels threatened by the talents or abilities of a female subordinate, and sets about putting her in her place by degrading or humiliating her.

Women who sexually harass men at work tend to have similar personality traits to those mentioned above. In particular they may feel a deep undercurrent of resentment and anger towards men, and may take the opportunity of being in an authoritative role to demean or ridicule a male worker, particularly if he is young, appears vulnerable or is isolated.

Case Study: Lynn, eighteen-year-old hairdresser

'It was my first job. I'd just left school and I was so thrilled to be training as a hairdresser. There were four other girls working with me. The owner was in his forties. The other girls warned me about him. Each of them told me a different story – that he'd groped them a few times, and promised them special treatment if they slept with him. I thought they were exaggerating, but I was still a bit wary of him.

One evening he asked me to stay behind to help with the last few customers. When everyone had gone, he locked the door, came over to where I was standing, and grabbed me from behind. He had his arms around me and he kept touching me. I told him to stop it. He said something like, "Sure we're only having a little fun. There's nothing wrong with that, is there?" He kept squeezing me, but I managed to push him away. Then he started laughing. "You'll have to get used to it," he said. "It's part of your duties. There are hundreds of girls out there who'd love a chance like I've given you, so just remember that!"

My mind was in a daze. I really felt shocked and frightened. I finished sweeping up the floor. He kept watching me. My face was bright red. Then I went to get my coat. "Will you come out for a drink this evening?" he said, as he stood, blocking my way out. "I've got to go home. My boyfriend is picking me up," I said. I was feeling really scared in case he wouldn't let me go. "Well just give me a kiss before I let you out." He grabbed me again and tried to kiss me. I pulled away from him. "I have to go," I kept saying. He looked a bit annoyed then. "I'll expect a better response next time," he said. Then he unlocked the door and let me out.

I felt so used. He'd treated me like I was nothing. I cried when I got home and I just couldn't stop. I wanted this job so much, but the thought of having to put up with that everyday made me feel really sick. I was really in bits. I told my family I'd had a row with my boss. I'm sorry now I didn't tell everyone the truth. Then I'd never have gone back. But I did go back for another few months. I just tried to avoid him as much as I could, and to always stay where the customers were. He tried it on a few more times. He really believed he owned us, that he could do anything he liked with us, just because he was paying our wages. We all worked so hard for the few miserable pounds he gave us. Any time he grabbed me I felt I'd lost another bit of my self. He had taken something away from me. I was so glad to get another job. I'm still sorry that I didn't do anything about it. I feel guilty, because he's probably giving other girls the same treatment.'

Lack of management training in people skills
It seems quite absurd that one of the most complex and vital skills in any organisation, that of managing people, is so often relegated to the bottom of the priority list in many Irish firms. How many managers or supervisors can we call to mind at will who have never even had one day's training in management? It is as though bestowing the title of manager on an accountant, or that of supervisor on a shop-worker, or that of foreman on an electrician, will magically equip the newly promoted with copious people skills, with conflict-resolutions skills, with the ability to motivate and delegate, and with the moral character and the maturity to take responsibility for the health and welfare of an entire department!

There is little doubt that supervisors and managers need to be educated and constantly monitored as to their treatment of workers who report to them. A manager who feels out of his or her depth from lack of training may suffer from high stress levels, generated by lack of knowledge and fear of failure. This kind of pressure may bring out behaviour in a newly-appointed manager which is uncharacteristic, such as bullying and intimidation of workers. Without having an awareness of the damaging effects caused by the misuse and abuse of power, and without having a positive support network to train and guide them, those who are promoted to managerial positions often fall straight into the arms of the old adage: power corrupts, and absolute power corrupts absolutely!

The perils of placing power in the hands of those who have not been specifically trained to cope with it have been well researched and documented. One of the best illustrations of this is Zimbardo's experiment, conducted in 1975. College students, who were deemed to have balanced personalities before the experiment, were selected and randomly assigned the roles of either prisoner or guard in a mock prison. The experiment had to be discontinued, however, before it was due to finish because the 'prisoners' had become so depressed and demoralised by the aggressive and authoritarian behaviour of the 'guards'. Since the only difference between the students was the role assigned to each, the subsequent abuse of power by the 'guards' suggested that, without a good deal of training and monitoring, even psychologically balanced individuals could readily abuse positions of power.

No organisation policy established on combating harassment
Employers are under a legal obligation to establish a set of disciplinary and grievance procedures, to ensure equitable treatment for employees if disputes arise. Although not legally binding, a code for dealing with sexual harassment was issued by the Department of Equality and Law Reform in September 1994. An employer is expected to do everything possible to prevent harassment from occurring at work.

In November 1992, the Dublin Rape Crisis Centre conducted a survey into the attitude of personnel professionals of firms, both large and small, to sexual harassment in their own organisations. Of those who responded, 70% were working in a company without a specific policy on sexual harassment, in contravention of a Labour Court ruling. Of the personnel professionals who were aware of reported incidents of sexual harassment in their own organisations, 70% had no training as to how to handle such incidents.

In the case of bullying, under Section 6 of the Safety, Health and Welfare at Work Act (1989), there is a duty on every employer to ensure, as far as is reasonable, the safety, health and welfare at work of all employees. An employer may be held liable under this act if bullying of an employee takes place at work, and a case is taken against the employer

When an organisation does not have any policy on sexual harassment or bullying, it leaves its staff wide-open to abuse and victimisation. When workers are not educated as to what constitutes harassment, and where there is a general feeling that a complaint of harassment will not be taken seriously, or may even lead to further victimisation, then the whole approach of the organisation to the welfare of its employees must be questioned.

Inadequate safeguards against stress and violence
Employers have a duty of care under the 1989 Health, Safety and Welfare at Work Act, which obliges them to identify and safeguard against all risks to health and safety. Controlling workplace stress is therefore no more optional for employers than the control of any other hazards.

Violence should also be considered a potential hazard and properly assessed. Where there is a risk to health and safety from violence, appropriate safeguards must be put into place. Under the Welfare at Work (General Application) Regulations, 1993, employers are required to ensure the safety and health of their employers. A safety statement should be drawn-up by finding out if there is a problem and how serious it is. This includes identifying the hazards, assessing the risks to health and safety, and then putting in place appropriate safeguards. The health and safety authority has identified certain key-areas where workers are most likely to be under threat from violence:

* Employees who work alone may be at greater risk and may feel more vulnerable to violence
* Job-location: where employees are mobile and may be working in areas which have a history of violent incidents
* Handling cash
* Working with members of the public, especially when people have to queue which can cause frustration
* Working at certain times of the day or night which are more dangerous than others, e.g. after pubs close, or when opening or closing premises in which cash is kept. (*Violence at work*)

Employers who do not provide appropriate safeguards to protect their staff from the effects of stressful work conditions, or from the threat of violence, may be liable to pay damages under the Safety, Health and Welfare at Work Act (1989), or the Welfare at Work (General Application) Regulations, (1993).

Summary: Signs of a dysfunctional workplace
The following is a list of symptoms which are frequently encountered in a boss-managed workplace:

* Managers make no attempt to praise, affirm or motivate staff
* Communication is poor or non-existent. Team members rarely meet with their manager to discuss goals, and are never consulted as to desirable work practices
* Suggestions, new ideas and creativity are discouraged, and rarely rewarded

* Constructive criticism of a manager's methods or decisions is construed as personal criticism
* There is no training of managers or supervisors in human resources
* Sexism, racism, favouritism, cliques and spy networks are all an integral part of the workplace
* Your boss is either (a) an autocratic, vindictive, abusive or angry personality, who bullies others to get his/her own way, or (b) a weak, incompetent, self-serving character who avoids confrontation at all costs, and who never takes responsibility for the staff's welfare
* Unions are outlawed. Total and absolute 'blind' loyalty to the firm is required of all staff
* Memos are constantly circulated by personnel, warning staff that breach of the latest company rule will lead to disciplinary action. Certain 'favoured' members of staff openly disregard the rules and are never disciplined
* Selected members of staff are persistently ridiculed, threatened, intimidated, criticised or isolated, on the whim of one or more powerful individuals
* Promotion is based on who you know and not on what you know
* Staff are too frightened to approach management or personnel to air grievances, for fear of victimisation
* No policy is issued to staff on the firm's commitment to combat sexual harassment and bullying at work
* Levels of staff turnover and absenteeism are extremely high
* Staff constantly feel anxious, stressed-out, and on the verge of burnout from striving to meet impossible deadlines, or unreasonable objectives
* Staff feel they have no control over their work, and become frustrated, fearful and apathetic

At National Level

High levels of unemployment
Turning our attention to the macrocosm, we are all familiar with the quarter-of-a-million people who are unemployed in Ireland. The fact that so many are unable to find work means that it is an employer's market in many sectors of the economy. Workers who are employed in organisations where harassment is rife are therefore more likely not to report it, for fear of victimisation or dismissal.

This is particularly true for workers who are aged over forty. A culture of youth, with the ideal age of workers being over twenty and less than forty, has rapidly developed a foothold in the Irish workplace. Workers aged fifty-plus often find themselves in a very vulnerable position, especially in a boss-managed firm. They are routinely selected for redundancies, and are also more likely to be bullied.

Women's vulnerable position in society
According to *Women in the labour force*, published by the Employment Equality Agency in September 1995, women accounted for 34.2% of the labour force in 1993. Female representation is highest in the following categories: clerical workers (78.23%), shop assistants and bar staff (59.59%), textile and clothing workers (58.47%), service workers (57.98%), and professional and technical workers (50.89%). Average gross earnings by women in manufacturing and industry (per hour) in 1993 was £4.94, compared with men's rates of £6.92 in manufacturing and £7.07 in industry.

The report emphasised that, despite advances in employment equality legislation, women still tend to be concentrated in low paid, part-time work. There are almost three times as many females engaged in regular part-time work as there are males. When we review the percentage of women in particular grades in the civil service (in 1992), women account for 94% of cleaning staff, 81% of clerical assistants, and 0% of the top secretary grades. In the local authorities, women occupy 98.94% of clerical, and 0% of city or assistant manager positions. With regard to professions, women account for 20.8% of membership of accountancy bodies (1994), and 35% of solicitors registered with the Law Society of Ireland (August 1995). Women accounted for a mere 18.95% of total administrative, executive and managerial workers (1993) across all sectors in Ireland.

Examining the figures for sexual harassment as researched by the Industrial Society in the UK, it is surely no coincidence that nine of out ten of those who reported being sexually harassed were female. Women's tendency to be employed in low graded and low paid employment, across all sectors, and given the propensity of harassment to occur most often as a result of a power-imbalance, makes women particularly vulnerable to being bullied and sexually harassed in the course of their employment.

When we look at the wider social issues, we find that many Irish women are subject to violence and abuse in their homes and within their communities. The Rape Crisis Centre counselled 515 survivors of rape and abuse between July 1996 and June 1997. 92% of these were women. (Rape Crisis Centre: *96-97 Statistics and financial summary*) Margaret Costelloe, co-ordinator of the Irish Federation of Women's Refuges, compiled statistics of the number of women who contacted their 13 refuges in 1997, due to violence in the home: 11,400 distress calls were received and 1,178 women sought accommodation. According to Kate Shanahan, in *Crimes worse than death*, violence against women is extremely prevalent in Ireland. Many crimes are never reported, so that the above figures are just the tip of the iceberg.

Put in this context, sexual harassment in the workplace is a mere symptom of the lack of respect for women in our society as a whole. An awareness of women's vulnerable position in the workplace should lead to more preventative measures being taken to combat sexual harassment and bullying, and more sensitive treatment of those who are the victims of harassment.

Inadequate legislation
Although legislation is in place, making it unlawful to subject an employee to sexual harassment (Employment Equality Act 1977), or bullying (Section 6 of the Safety, Health and Welfare at Work Act 1989), further legislation making it compulsory for employers to issue policy statements on harassment to all employees is absolutely necessary and long overdue. Many workers are not aware of what constitutes sexual harassment or bullying at work. Nor are many familiar with the legal requirements for employers to ensure that stressful working conditions are not allowed to prevail in any workplace.

All workers have a right to be informed about current Irish legislation regarding employees' rights in protecting them from harassment. This could be issued along with the initial contract of employment. Each member of staff should likewise be educated as to a proper code of conduct which is appropriate to the workplace. Employees who are members of trade unions have access to this information and have a built-in support network to advise and support them if they are experiencing harassment.

Where membership of a trade union is outlawed by an organisation, individual or collective workers may find themselves intimidated if they express the wish to join a union.

Although it is a constitutional right for any Irish citizen to join a union, legislation is still needed to ensure that workers can be represented by their union in cases of disputes between employees and employers. The latter has access to employer confederations, to personnel, and to legal professionals, while the only representation most workers have is their union. Without the right to union representation, workers may feel a great deal of fear and intimidation when contemplating making a formal complaint of bullying or harassment at work, or when required to give evidence during an investigation into alleged harassment.

CHAPTER FOUR

Effects of harassment on employees

I. EFFECTS OF SEXUAL HARASSMENT

Sexual harassment infringes the basic dignity of the individual, and can have a devastating effect on the health, competence, morale and self-esteem of those affected. Workers who are being sexually harassed often feel powerless, frightened, demeaned, angry, humiliated, and isolated. Many feel they will be blamed for causing the unwanted behaviour if they report the abuse, so they remain silent. Others feel frightened that they will be demoted, suffer further victimisation or dismissal if they speak out. Feelings of anxiety and stress, loss of confidence, and bouts of illness are common experiences of those who are sexually harassed. A person's social life and personal relationships may also be adversely affected.

Victims often report feeling 'dirty', 'demeaned', and 'used', particularly if the harassment has been physical in nature. Those who are coerced into giving sexual favours for fear of losing their jobs, frequently feel angry, guilty, and violated. Often the victim is forced to leave employment without having secured another position, which can cause short and long term financial hardship. Where the harassment is particularly vicious or prolonged, including sexual assault and rape, the victim may experience bouts of severe depression and suicidal thoughts.

Although the majority of victims of sexual harassment are women, men may also find themselves becoming the butt of sexual jokes, and unwanted physical contact. Men have also reported being groped and teased at work by male and female colleagues. It can be particularly difficult for a male victim of harassment to come forward and seek support, due to the fear of appearing 'weak' or 'un-macho' to workmates.

Case studies of sexual harassment

Laurie: nineteen-year-old legal secretary

When Laurie obtained her National Certificate in Legal Studies, she was over the moon to be employed by a small firm of solicitors. She was nineteen years old. She got herself a flat and borrowed the cost of the deposit from her parents. The firm was run by three partners. There were seven people employed in all. Laurie and Sharon, the other secretary, were the only two females employed. Within a few weeks of working there, the senior partner began to make comments to Laurie which she felt very uncomfortable about.

'You're a very pretty little thing,' he said to her one afternoon when she met him on the corridor. 'I'd like to see you wearing a shorter skirt, though,' he winked at her and then walked away.

Laurie was disturbed by this and other personal comments made to her by this partner. She asked Sharon tentatively how she was treated by the partners, and was told, 'The other two are all right, but just watch the senior guy – he's woman mad! I'm OK though because I'm married and on the other side of thirty.'

Laurie felt very uneasy anytime she saw the senior partner. He seemed to be always staring at her, sneering and looking her up and down. One evening when she'd been asked by another of the partners to stay behind and do some extra filing, the senior partner followed her into the filing room.

'At last! Would you do me a favour and pick out a file for me. The name is ....'

Laurie nervously turned towards the filing cabinet. The next thing she knew she was grabbed from behind and pinned to the cabinet. He was rubbing up against her. He was breathing hard and he had his hand up her skirt. Laurie froze momentarily. Then she heard herself screaming, 'Let me alone, get away from me.' She pulled herself away from him.

'You won't get far here with that attitude,' he growled at her.

Laurie ran out of the filing room, pulled her coat from the rack, and went out into the street. She couldn't stop crying. What would she do now? She couldn't face ever going to work there again, that was for sure. She didn't want to tell anyone what had happened. She had some knowledge of labour law from her studies but she wasn't in a union, and she couldn't face confronting the senior partner of a law firm with the accusation of sexual harassment.

Laurie sent a letter of resignation the following morning. She gave notice on her flat, and decided to go for counselling to deal with the trauma and the feelings of powerlessness she was experiencing. She returned home to recuperate. It was not until six months later that she began looking for further employment.

Anne: fifty-one-year-old insurance clerk

Anne had worked as a clerk for the same company for over sixteen years. It was a large company with a very high profile. The first twelve years had passed without any major incidents, as Anne had a good working relationship with her immediate manager. He had always praised her work, and although the salary in the company was not over-generous, Anne felt quite fulfilled and happy in her employment. It was when her manager retired and a new manager, John, was appointed, that the trouble began.

From the outset John made disparaging comments about Anne's age. At this time, Anne was the only person employed in the company who was in her late forties. Anne was also single, and living with her sister. Several of the other clerks in Anne's department were not very long out of school. John began whispering things under his breath whenever Anne came into his office. Things like: 'It's a terrible penance to have to work with a frustrated spinster.' 'Early retirement should be compulsory for women when they lose their figure.' 'A woman without a man is an unnatural state of affairs.'

Anne did her best to ignore these comments although they were deeply embarrassing and hurtful. She was in no doubt that John's comments were directly aimed at her. He treated the younger women in a very different way, even promoting one girl to a position which Anne felt entitled to. Still, his comments to the younger women were also loaded with sexism: 'Good morning, cutie, you look really lovely today; that colour really accentuates your ... assets, love!' On one occasion he invited all of the female staff – except Anne – out for drinks after work on Friday evening. Anne did not hear about this until the following Monday morning.

Anne felt devastated by John's unfair treatment of her. She became more and more isolated from her co-workers. She began having difficulty sleeping, and felt sick each morning on wakening, as she now dreaded having to go to work. She felt powerless. She didn't have any savings, and at her time of life she

didn't think she'd realistically get another job. She felt very fearful that John would try to dismiss her from her job.

John criticised Anne's work at every possible opportunity.
He even humiliated her in front of junior staff, sniggering that
she was well past the sell-by date. Then his comments got even
nastier and more disturbing. One Monday morning, when Anne
returned to work after being out sick for a week, John called her
into his office and said, 'I suppose you spent most of the week in
bed – masturbating!'

Anne went beetroot with embarrassment. In all her adult
years she had never been spoken to in such a disgusting manner.
Anne walked out of the office and down to the ladies', where she
vomited in the toilet. There was no one in the company whom
she felt she could turn to. The personnel officer was known to be
very friendly with John, and to always take the side of management in any company dispute. There was no union in the firm,
as union membership was practically outlawed by senior management. Anne returned to her desk and tried to avoid John as
much as possible. That night she couldn't sleep. She visited her
GP, but was too embarrassed to tell him what had been said to
her. Anyway he mightn't believe her. He prescribed sleeping
tablets.

Over the next few months John's comments became even
more sexually explicit, and more disturbing. 'Would you like to
feel me inside of you sometime?' he whispered to Anne when
she was looking up a quote for him in the filing room. 'You'd be
surprised how big a man can get down there. If you ever want to
take a look then I can arrange it.' One day when she brought him
in some files he'd requested he touched her hand and said, 'I'm
sure your work would vastly improve if you had a good ride.'

Anne's friends noticed a major change in her personality. She
became edgy and would often lapse into long silences. Anne lost
her appetite and became pale and withdrawn. She felt trapped
and powerless. Over a period of two years she applied for several
jobs, but wasn't called for any interview. Her thoughts constantly
turned to work. She dreaded even seeing John. She couldn't bare
for him to look at her. Her confidence plummeted. She felt dirty
and used. There was no one she could confide in. She developed
an ulcer, and started to have panic attacks. After spending one
night walking the streets, seriously thinking about throwing
herself in the river, she realised she had to get help. She phoned
her local SIPTU branch. This was the first time she had ever told

anyone about her work situation. She felt such relief when Tom, the union official, explained she was being sexually harassed, and that she wasn't the first person to have experienced such appalling treatment in her workplace. Tom advised Anne to note the dates and the times of any further incidences, and to record if there were any witnesses present. He also advised Anne to do up a journal of past incidences, in as much detail as she could recall. Written details would be required for any action which Anne might choose to take against her employers.

At that time Anne felt far too scared to confront John, and she dreaded what would happen if the company discovered she was a member of a union. However, Anne had taken a brave step in telling Tom, the union official, what she had been suffering. Without Tom's support and encouragement Anne felt she would have had a complete breakdown. It was over a year later, when things became unbearable for Anne and her health was being seriously undermined by her appalling work situation, that Anne asked Tom to contact the company with a view to being compensated for all she had suffered at the hands of John. Anne was finally able to obtain a substantial settlement from the company.

David: seventeen-year-old laundry worker
'I had just turned seventeen when I got a job working in a laundry. Most of the staff were women, and were older than me. They gave me a terrible time right from the start. They kept talking about sex, what it was like with their husbands and boyfriends, and they kept glancing over at me to see my reaction. I felt so awkward and embarrassed. I used to wish the ground would open up and swallow me. Then they kept asking me had I a girlfriend, and what kind of girls I liked. I suppose I was fairly inexperienced and quiet. They really gave me a bad time.

There's one incident I'm still embarrassed about. It was lunchtime and I was in the queue in the canteen. A few of the women from my section were behind me and I could hear them all jeering me. All of a sudden one of the girls grabbed me and squeezed my balls. "He's got something there alright," she shouted to her friends. I was fit to explode I was so angry, but the worst thing was the embarrassment.

I couldn't stand going to work after that. I hated being laughed about. I had no gang of my own to back me up. I hated the way they kept jeering that I was a real stud. Then they'd laugh about how thin I was. Working in that laundry was a rough experience. I had no confidence when I left and tried looking for other jobs.'

Cathy: twenty-four-year-old lecturer
'I was employed on a contract basis by a third-level college as a junior lecturer. It was my first job. I was desperately trying to make a good impression with colleagues and students. My boss was very kind to me at first, saying his door was always open if I had any problems. I felt a little uncomfortable when he started staring at me and looking me up and down, but I really didn't put much pass on this. I mean, it's not a crime to find someone attractive. He was at least thirty years older than me, and I knew he was married, so I never thought I'd anything to worry about. It was only when my contract was up for renewal that I became wary of him.

He called me into his office one morning and said that I need have no worries about my contract because the sole decision to keep me on rested with him. He said he was certain I had a great career ahead of me, and he really enjoyed having me on his staff. Then out of the blue he said he'd like to discuss my contract over dinner at an exclusive restaurant. I was absolutely shocked. He got up from his desk, walked over to me and put his arm on my shoulder. I was aware that he was staring at my breasts. I said I'd think about it, thanked him for the invitation and told him I had a class to take. I didn't want to hurt his feelings, because this contract was so important to me. I still wanted to be on good terms with him.

After that episode he kept calling me in every morning, asking if I wanted him to sign the contract, and saying he'd be happy to do so over dinner. I put it off for weeks, but one day I'd had a really bad morning in class and when he called me in, I just agreed to go with him. He walked over behind me and rubbed his hand through my hair. He told me his wife was away that week. He said he'd arrange everything. I felt really scared.

He brought me to a beautiful restaurant. He was all fatherly to me, advising me to start studying for a Ph D, under his supervision. He said there was no problem about the contract, and he'd sign it the following morning. He said he just liked my company so much. Afterwards he asked me around to his home for coffee. I said no, I didn't feel that was appropriate. He kissed me on the cheek, and said I probably needed time to get used to the arrangement. I felt sick for allowing myself to be in such a predicament, but I wasn't going to let it go any further.

The next morning he signed my contract. He said he'd love to see me again. I said maybe sometime. I felt I needed the experience before I could go to another college, and I was afraid he might ruin my career if I confronted him. Over the next few months he kept asking me out, and the staring got worse. One lecturer called me aside and asked me if I was aware that my boss had developed an obsession for me. She said everyone was talking about it. I felt terrible inside. The next time he called me into his office I told him I'd got a boyfriend, and that I couldn't go out with him again. He seemed to be upset and angry, but he asked if we could still be friends. He still kept staring at me, and calling me in to his office. I began to look for other jobs. It was a demeaning experience. I wish it had never happened.'

II. EFFECTS OF BULLYING

It is a common experience for workers who are being systematically bullied to feel demeaned, inadequate, and deeply distressed. Many feel too embarrassed and ashamed to talk about what is going on in their work place. This is especially true for men, who find it very difficult to admit that they are being bullied, particularly if they work in a 'macho' environment. This fear of losing face for reporting bullying is even more pronounced when a man is being bullied by a female.

To many it feels that bullying is something which happens to a few unlucky kids at school and has no place in the adult world. It can be very difficult to understand what is happening, to realise that it is not the worker's own behaviour or attitude which is at fault. It is usual for the victim of this kind of prolonged harassment to suffer from self-doubt, and to wonder what he or she is doing to deserve this treatment. Constant petty criticism, and failure to meet impossible deadlines, eats away at self-esteem, eroding perhaps years of positive reviews and appreciative managers, stripping away layers of experience and competence, exposing our vulnerabilities. This is particularly the case when one worker is selected by a boss for victimisation and becomes isolated from co-workers who are too frightened themselves to take the side of the victim.

Bullying often starts when management selects a worker whom they no longer have any use for, and whom they want to force to resign. Work will be scrutinised and monitored, as the manager has been ordered to find 'legitimate' grounds for dismissal. There is desperate pressure inflicted on a person in this situation not to make mistakes. It becomes a nightmarish battle which the worker has no chance of winning, unless support from a union is sought.

The effects of bullying on a worker can be crippling. Feelings can include fear, impotence, powerlessness, anger, hatred, rage, and the desire to seek revenge. Workers may be so fearful of going to work that they may vomit and feel physically ill before leaving for work each morning. In many cases, a person's self-respect among colleagues and co-workers, and the means of his or her livelihood, are under siege by constant bullying and intimidation. This is particularly the case when a worker feels trapped and loses all hope of securing further employment due to age or a lack of skills and training. When our basic survival needs are threatened we usually experience feelings of terror. When self-respect is being systematically destroyed, and a person feels powerless to do anything to stop it, thoughts of suicide often enter the victim's mind. Actual suicides have occurred as a result of workplace bullying.

Case Studies of bullying

Paul, forty-five-year-old chef
'I've worked in hotels all over Europe for over thirty years. I began as kitchen porter and worked up through the ranks until I became chef. There's one hotel I worked in that I'll never forget. It was in the south of Ireland. The manager was diabolical. Everyone was afraid of him. When he lost his temper he cursed and shouted like a mad man. He was a tyrant, a complete bully. It was a simple case of power going to his head. He thought he had a God-given right to treat us like slaves, to walk all over us. There was no point complaining to personnel because they always sided with management. I stood up to him many times. I was reared to fight my own corner and to believe I was as good as anyone else. There were countless times he threatened to fire me. But I would have taken him to the ends of the earth if he'd dismissed me unfairly.

I'll never forget one incident. I'd worked flat-out all over Christmas, including St Stephen's day and New Year's Eve. I didn't trust him an inch, so I made sure to remind him to include the extra pay in my wages that he'd promised. He told me the hotel had been too quiet over Christmas and they couldn't afford to pay me. I nearly hit the roof. I contacted the department of employment and told them the story. Then I went back to the manager and told him I was taking him to the Labour Court if he didn't pay up. The next week I got the extra money, and he was all nice to me. He was a real coward once anyone stood up to him and he'd always back down.

Then there were the other complications. From time to time he'd sleep with one of the female staff, and that meant she'd get better money and more sociable working hours. I had desperately long hours. Sometimes I'd have to do a seventy or eighty hour week. I wasn't the only one in that boat. Sometimes there were major shouting matches that went on. You'd think it was more like a nut house than a hotel. He basically didn't like anyone. I really think he had a mental problem. I know he was on the verge of alcoholism and he split up with his wife just before I left. I've seen some bad places over the years but that place took the biscuit.'

Suzy, twenty-seven-year-old staff nurse
'I worked in a psychiatric hospital for three years. My boss, Mr Black, was the head nurse on the ward. I initially got on with him OK. Then I witnessed an incident which greatly shocked me. I saw him hurting a patient who'd thrown a temper tantrum. He grabbed her, put her into a cold bath, pulled her by the hair, and banged her head off the taps. I felt so guilty for not reporting that incident. He acted as though this kind of behaviour was quite normal. I was extremely wary of him after that. A couple of students also came to me and said they'd seen him stealing patients' belongings. I kept all of this in my head, but I was too scared to confront him directly.

Then another incident occurred. I had been on holidays, and on my return I discovered that Mr Black had taken his annual leave. On his strict instructions I was to continue treating an old lady, Anne, who had severe brain damage and who had the mental capacity of a two-year old. He said it had been agreed at a case conference that this woman should be let walk around the town freely, with a nurse following some distance behind, to see if she'd be able to cope on her own. According to the nurses who had already been involved in this 'treatment', Anne would walk across roads without looking, and it was only luck that she hadn't been killed. I was appalled at this disregard for Anne's safety. If anything happened to Anne I would be accountable. I therefore stopped his 'treatment'.

When Mr Black returned he screamed at me for daring to disobey his instructions, and he threatened to have me dismissed. I was scared and very upset. I just knew he was wrong. I couldn't work under such a controlling and bullying supervisor any longer. My only avenue was to go to our overall boss. It transpired that my boss knew nothing about Mr Black's treatment of Anne. It had all been lies that a case conference had made the decision on Anne's care. My boss told me that loads of people had left because they couldn't work with Mr Black, due to his bullying attitude and behaviour. An actual case conference was held, and the doctors, the social workers, and the psychiatric staff were all outraged that this dangerous 'treatment' had been inflicted on Anne. Mr Black was forced to resign and was blacklisted from ever working in any hospital in the area.'

Peter: Nineteen-year-old electrical apprentice
Peter worked with four other electrical apprentices in a factory which manufactured computer parts. The foreman there was noted for being a hard man, especially with new workers. Right from the first day he gave abusive nick-names to the four apprentices, and told them he'd make life hell for anyone who wasn't up to scratch. Peter had loved working with electricity since he was a kid. It came natural to him. He was extremely conscientious and would always manage to get a job finished in half the time of any other worker. It came as a great shock to Peter when the foreman started jeering him in front of the others, calling him a show-off and describing his work as 'shoddy'. This went on hour after hour. He'd come up and stand behind Peter, staring over his shoulder when he was trying to do his work. This completely unnerved Peter. Once he asked the foreman could he see him in private. The foreman shouted, 'No way! You're not wasting my time. Get back to your shoddy work,' and then followed another tirade of abuse.

Peter felt his hands shaking every time he saw the foreman approaching. He couldn't concentrate on his work, and began to slow down, to double-check everything he was doing. He became terrified of making mistakes because he figured he'd surely be crucified if he made even the slightest slip. Peter started to have difficulty sleeping. Within three weeks of working at the factory he started to feel sick most mornings before going to work, and developed piercing headaches. Peter started to talk to a few of the other workers and found out that they too were terrified of the foreman. They told him there was a huge staff turnover in their section. He began to realise that the foreman probably had it in for him because he was so interested in his work, and he'd set out to destroy him. Within a month Peter had secured another apprenticeship, but it took him many months to regain his old confidence.

Josephine, forty-five-year-old financial analyst
'I had over twenty years experience, both in Ireland and abroad, working as a financial analyst, before joining a large Dublin company. I had seven members of staff reporting to me. I'd been working there a few months when I was approached by my boss, and asked to investigate a case of suspected embezzlement in my department.

I painstakingly checked through cashier transaction records, and my suspicion fell on one girl in particular. I wrote a detailed report for my boss, but since there was no absolute evidence, I didn't disclose any names. My boss called me in late one Friday afternoon and demanded to know the name of the person I suspected. I replied that I couldn't do this, as I had no wish to blacken the name of any staff member without solid proof. My boss said he was disappointed in my unhelpful attitude, and that he'd report the matter to the chief executive.

After this incident, things began to deteriorate rapidly. My boss was decidedly cool when he spoke to me. I was called into his office a few weeks later, and this time I was told to keep a close eye on my staff and report back if I discovered that any of them were involved in a union. I was shocked by this request, and replied that spying on fellow staff was not part of my job description. He shouted, 'Who the hell do you think you are?' He said if I had any aspirations of further promotion I'd better collect plenty of relevant information for the CE. I couldn't believe this was happening to me. I was visibly shaking and there were tears in my eyes when I left his office. He'd reduced me to the size of a snivelling child. I felt so angry and upset.

A number of incidents followed. When it was time for my annual review, I was informed that I wasn't getting an increase. In fact, my salary was frozen. I protested to personnel but got no satisfaction. Then one Monday morning after returning from

holidays my boss told me I was being moved to a more appropriate location. This office was much smaller and was located at
the back of the building. It had no window. The last straw came
when a few weeks later an intricate and complex section of my
work was removed from me, and given to a junior member of
my own department who was subsequently promoted.

After this incident, life became a sheer misery. My office door
had glass panels in it, and one morning I nearly fainted with the
fright when I saw the CE staring in at me. I felt like an animal
trapped in a cage, being teased by the circus master. This became a most intimidating feature of my working life, made all
the more unsettling by its unpredictable nature. For the first
time in my life I became terrified of making mistakes. I kept
checking figures over and over, in case I'd give my boss the ex-
cuse to demote or dismiss me. I kept thinking back to previous
positions I'd had, where my work was highly praised and rewarded.

I find it difficult to begin to describe the feelings of fear and
anxiety I experienced during that time. The staff realised I'd lost
favour, so they lost respect for me. Any of the managers whom I
had been friendly with simply didn't want to know. I had been
black-listed so I was bad news. People walked the other way
when they saw me coming. I even heard members of staff talking about me in the ladies', speculating as to what I must have
done to be punished in such a way.

I began to feel really depressed. I knew it would take me a
long time to find another position at my age. At the time I didn't
understand what was happening to me. I lost all confidence in
myself. I felt physically sick most days. I chain-smoked sixty cigarettes in the evenings. I was prescribed sleeping tablets by my
GP, but most nights they didn't work. I could only sleep a few
hours, and would usually wake up at two or three in the morning.
I'd often get dressed then and even have breakfast at four in the
morning. The fear of demotion, and the thought that my career
could be ruined, nearly drove me demented. For the first time in
my life I really felt powerless. I ran up huge bills ringing friends,
telling them about the situation at work. It became an obsession.
I had never known such terror before. I felt trapped, and I'm
ashamed to admit it but I even had thoughts of ending it all.
Then there were the feelings of anger and revenge. I'd have
loved to lock my boss away in a damp dark cell where he'd be
whipped and tortured. I had nightmares about my boss and the

CE, in which they were hounding me, and hysterically laughing about me.

The pressure finally got too much for me. I went sick for several months. I can't see myself ever going back there again. I've started to apply for other positions. I'll never forget the injustice and the terrible misery I endured in that despicable place.'

Joe: eighteen-year-old navy cadet

Joe was eighteen when he joined the navy. He was stationed in Cobh to undergo his basic training. Right from the start he was singled out because of his West of Ireland accent. A large crowd of Dublin lads, who were training with him, constantly jeered him and called him every abusive name under the sun. Joe became the butt of every joke. Some evenings the jeering turned to violence, and Joe was pushed, thumped and kicked around the room. Most times they'd draw blood before they'd finish.

Other nights his bunk would be upended. There was no supervision in the barracks, so if any one wanted to let off steam then they could do as they pleased. A few other guys also had a desperate time. Joe felt so isolated and fearful that at times he couldn't speak when he was in a group of more than three or four. He felt humiliated and his confidence was destroyed. He didn't dare tell the officers what was happening because the other lads would surely kill him if he did. He felt trapped, like he was in prison, with no one to turn to. The actual physical training wasn't any problem to him, but he knew he couldn't take much more abuse or many more beatings. He developed stomach problems and didn't feel like eating. He was too frightened to sleep, in case the gang would jump on him in the middle of the night. If he did fall asleep he'd wake up shaking and perspiring. Joe was discharged on health grounds before he had completed six months of training.

III. EFFECTS OF VIOLENCE

Bullying may involve physical violence being perpetrated against a worker, such as pushing, punching, kicking or slapping, by a colleague or superior. Emotionally, victims of violent bullying often feel deeply shocked, angry, frightened and out of control. There are workers who have been intimidated by employers with the threat of physical violence to self and to relatives, if they dare to involve a union or to take a case against the firm.

This type of bullying is criminal, and the effects on those concerned are long-lasting, severely damaging and deeply traumatic.

Violence may also be inflicted on workers by members of the public. The physical effects of violence can range from cuts and bruises, to broken bones and life-threatening injuries, which may leave the victim scarred or disabled. Serious assault, even resulting in death, has become a real fear for many types of workers in the course of their duties. Occupations most vulnerable to attack are those who enforce the law (e.g. gardaí, army, wardens, social workers), those who handle money (e.g. security workers, cashiers, bus drivers, shop assistants), and those who work in the caring professions (e.g. nurses). Working in areas where there is a likelihood of violence can lead to low staff morale and high levels of stress. (*Guidance on the prevention of violence at work*, 1995)

The psychological effects of violence on employees include anxiety, helplessness, irritability, soreness, hyper alertness, sadness, depression, and shock. This type of reaction is referred to as post traumatic stress disorder, and can include constant thoughts about the incident, muscle tenseness, fatigue, increased use of alcohol, nicotine and food as a means of coping (Poster and Ryan, 1993)

The Health and Safety Authority has reported injuries to workers which necessitated surgery, and which led to long term disability. A major psychological effect of violence is the loss of self-confidence. Unless this is adequately treated, it may develop into behavioural problems, anxiety, depression, or post traumatic stress disorder. (*Violence at work*)

Case Study: Violence

Theresa, twenty-one-year-old shop assistant
'I'd been working in a supermarket for a few months. It was a fairly busy place. Four of us would be on from seven in the morning till four in the evening. I'll never forget that morning. It was wintry and cold. It was about 11.30. I was at the cash register when these two men rushed in the door and ran over to me, screaming to give them money. I froze with the shock. One of them had an iron bar. I was fumbling with the register, trying to open it. Just as it sprung open I felt a terrible pain in my back, and I fell to the floor. I'd been hit a few times with the iron bar. I curled up in a ball on the floor and covered my head. I thought

they'd kill me. I can't describe the terror I felt. Someone finally ran over to me and said they'd gone. I couldn't stop crying. The pain was really severe. Someone rang the boss and he told me to take the rest of the day off. He said he needed me in the next morning though, because one of the girls was on holidays.

I cried for hours. I went to the hospital to get an x-ray. The doctor said there was no real damage, just bruising. Still the pain wouldn't go away. I went in to work the following day. I couldn't sit at the register. I was too scared. I was moved to the deli counter. No one ever mentioned taking time off. I never got a penny in compensation. But that one incident changed my whole life. I really withdrew into my self. I didn't want to walk alone in the street, even in the day time. I looked on everyone as an enemy. I hadn't done anything wrong but I'd been attacked for no reason. I split up with my boyfriend. He was understanding at first but then he was annoyed because I felt scared even going into a pub. I just wanted to blend into the background. I felt so exposed and vulnerable.

I took a lot of sick days. I was chided by the supervisor over that. I just couldn't cope. I finally left the job. I couldn't work with the public any more. It was about a year after the assault and the pain in my back wasn't getting any better. The doctor said it was all in my mind. He recommended I attend a counsellor. It helped me a lot to talk to someone who really understood how I was feeling. I'm just angry now that my boss never once asked me how the assault had affected me, and never even offered to pay for my medical and counselling expenses.'

IV. EFFECTS OF STRESS

According to the health and safety authority, workers who endure excessively stressful conditions often experience anxiety and fatigue. They are more prone to making mistakes and having accidents. They are more likely to indulge in excessive smoking, drinking, eating or drug-taking. High levels of stress over a long period of time have been shown to contribute to heart-disease, reduced resistance to infection, digestive problems and skin problems. Striving to meet impossible deadlines or to complete excessive amounts of work often leaves workers feeling anxious, inadequate, frustrated, depressed, and out of control. (*Workplace stress: Cause, effects and control*)

Case Study: Stress

Michael, nineteen-year-old trainee accountant

'I had passed my first level accountancy exams in college before being taken on by a small accountancy firm down the country. It was my first job. I was thrown in at the deep end. I was given five or six cases to work on, concurrently. The rest of the staff seemed very strained and over-worked. Wages were minimal, and no over-time was paid, but most of the trainees would put in a fifty-hour week, just barely trying to keep ahead of the deadlines. The boss was a tough man, to say the least. He'd call a meeting on the last Friday of every month. I remember the scene: the boss sitting at the top of the room, the two partners sitting one at either side, and then all the terrified trainees sitting there, eyes cast to the ground. I used to shake with sheer terror in case he'd call my name. I saw him verbally rip grown men to shreds, in front of the entire staff.

Unless you were a friend or relation there's no way you'd escape. My day of shame finally dawned. He'd given me a whole set of accounts to complete in just three days. He'd warned me I'd better have them done, because he had to attend an appeal at the end of the week. I was too scared to say I couldn't do it. I stayed at work until nine or ten each night. I finished the accounts, but I'm sure I had made a few mistakes. I mean I'd done two to three weeks' work in three days. But he pulled me asunder in front of the whole staff. I never felt so small in my life. I could hardly speak to defend myself. Afterwards I really wished I was dead. There's nothing more I could have done to do a better job. I felt worse because I'd really tried. That destroyed my confidence. I wanted to go somewhere and hide. The other staff were too embarrassed to say anything, so they more or less avoided me for the rest of the day.

After that incident I was a complete wreck. I developed a chest infection, but I knew I had to go to work. I couldn't face food. I had a knot in my stomach every morning. I felt sick. Most nights I couldn't sleep. I believed I needed that job if I ever wanted to qualify. I kept going over the books in my mind, trying to come up with solutions to problems, even if it was four in the morning. Every time I saw the boss coming into the room I felt a stab of fear in my gut. We were all severely stressed-out. There was a complete lack of morale, because no matter what you did you knew he could still tear it in halves, and fling it on the floor.

I saw him doing that once to a guy. I know it sounds ridiculous but I really thought it was the way all bosses behaved. I never once thought that he was at fault. It was only when I finally managed to get out of there that I realised he was a monster, on some kind of power-trip.'

SUMMARY

In summary, the following psychological effects have been reported by workers who have experienced sexual harassment, bullying, violence and stress in the workplace:
* Physical problems manifesting, such as aches and pains, migraine, backache, ulcers, skin disorders, stomach problems, loss of appetite, nausea and vomiting, which may necessitate periods of sick-leave
* Difficulty sleeping
* Obsessive thoughts about work
* Emotional exhaustion
* Bouts of uncontrollable sobbing
* Palpitations, panic attacks and mood swings
* Feeling inadequate, powerless and out of control
* Loss of sex-drive, sometimes leading to impotence
* Emotional withdrawal from family, friends and colleagues
* Feeling unmotivated, lethargic and apathetic
* Increased reliance on drugs, cigarettes, and alcohol
* Feeling anxious, fearful and irritable
* Lacking confidence and self-esteem
* Feeling shocked and bewildered, humiliated and demeaned
* Fear of making mistakes, which leads to a decrease in job performance
* Feeling depressed, accompanied by thoughts of suicide, attempted suicide or actual suicide
* Feeling alienated, frozen out and isolated
* Feeling anger and hatred towards the harasser
* Daydreaming of taking revenge and getting even
* Unfair dismissal
* Constructive dismissal due to severity of harassment
* Leaving employment before another job has been secured.

CHAPTER FIVE

Effects of harassment and bullying on organisations

High levels of absenteeism and labour turnover
In England, about 300 million working days are lost through absenteeism each year, which works out at an average per employee per year of 13.5 days. (Argyle, 1989, p. 250) Uncertified absenteeism has been estimated to account for up to half of all absenteeism. (Chadwick-Jones *et al*, 1982) Figures obtained from the Department of Employment in the UK indicate that the financial cost to British industry of sickness absence caused by stress and mental disorders is between £1 and £5 billion each year. *(Bullying at work, BBC)* High levels of absenteeism tend to occur when job satisfaction and general working conditions are poor.

In Ireland the Health and Safety Authority (HSA) has highlighted the effects of excessive levels of stress on organisations. These include increased absenteeism, low motivation, reduced productivity, reduced efficiency, faulty decision making, and poor industrial relations. *(Workplace Stress)* The effects of violence on firms have also been emphasised by the HSA. Violence will lower staff morale, and may make it difficult to recruit and retain new staff. It will also increase costs due to absenteeism, employer's liability premiums and compensation. *(Violence at work)*

A report on absenteeism in the public service in Ireland was commissioned by the Department of the Public Service in 1986. The civil service, local authorities, state-sponsored bodies, and the health services were included in the commission. Absenteeism was defined as time lost attributable to sickness or any other cause not excused through statutory entitlements or conditions of employment. In summary, the commission found that out of a staff of 25,500 civil servants:
* 195,405 days were lost in the proceeding year through sick-leave: this was an average of 7.66 days per person
* 57% of the total days lost through sick leave were attributable to only 10% of the staff
* It was found that work-related factors had a large bearing on

absenteeism. Workers who had the poorest attendance records also tended to work in areas where job satisfaction was low, and there was a large number of staff in each work unit. Working conditions were physically unpleasant, and understaffing frequently occurred which over-burdened staff. There was a high workload at peak times, and the nature of the job was routine and monotonous. The degree of skill required to do the job and the level of responsibility was low. The organisational structure of the workplace was hierarchical, and there was little or no participation or consultation with staff. (Blennerhassett and Gorman, 1986)

Average levels of labour turnover are in the region of 20 to 25% annually. (Mowday *et al*, 1982) Excessively high levels of labour turnover strongly indicate a severe workplace problem. The cost for most organisations of recruiting and training new staff is very high, in terms of time and money. The constant loss of experienced and knowledgeable workers causes major headaches for firms. The problem of recruiting staff has been recently exacerbated by the shortage of highly skilled workers in many industries. The Irish Small and Medium Enterprises Association (ISME) carried out a survey recently. (*The Irish Times*, 15 Sept 1997) Out of thirty multinationals, only two had no labour or skills shortage, while twenty-eight had. Out of sixty-nine small and medium sized firms, only nine had no labour shortage, while sixty had.

Factors found to cause high levels of labour turnover are low job satisfaction, poor pay and conditions, problems with supervisors or colleagues, and lack of commitment to the organisation. (Argyle, 1989, p. 255-257) In the case of an employee who is being harassed, work can become a nightmare. Any previous job satisfaction quickly evaporates. Acute stress, low morale, and a whole host of emotional symptoms are rampant. Without the proper channels to air grievances, and the assurance that the matter will be dealt with in a confidential and fair manner, many workers are left with little option but to seek alternative employment.

Low productivity
Bullying and sexual harassment affect workers' morale, and hence productivity, according to Dr Tom Donnelly, Occupational Advisor with the Health and Safety Authority. (*The Examiner*, 2 December 1997, p. 5) In Ireland we have hardly begun to quantify

in monetary terms the loss in productivity to businesses due to harassment. In the USA, for example, the Bureau of National Affairs states that firms are losing as much as five to six billion dollars in decreased productivity due to real or perceived abuse. (*Personnel Journal*, July 1991)

Research into the causes of loss of productivity in the workplace may come as startling news to those organisations which rely on fear and coercion to control workers. Rensis Likert, director of the Institute of Social Research at the University of Michigan, USA, conducted several studies into workers' motivation, and its effect on productivity levels in the workplace. His research indicated that managers and supervisors who promoted co-operative and supportive relationships at work, and who gave employees the opportunity for self-fulfilment, creativity, and economic security, tended to achieve the highest productivity, the lowest costs and the highest levels of employee motivation.

According to Likert, participative group management is the ideal system, where productivity is excellent, and where absenteeism and staff-turnover are extremely low. The ethos of this type of management is participation, co-operation, communication at all levels, commitment to achieving common goals, and staff incentives which are both economically and psychologically desirable.

Other researchers in this field (Iaffaldano and Muchinsky, 1985; and Petty *et al*, 1984) found a positive correlation between job satisfaction and productivity levels. Workers therefore tend to work harder when they feel contented and valued at work.

According to IBEC, although it is impossible to guess the cost to employers of harassment in the workplace, there is little doubt that bullying poses a major indirect, unnecessary and unwanted cost to businesses, primarily in terms of low morale and productivity, poor work performance, absenteeism, labour turnover and minor illnesses. (*Workplace bullying*, 1996) Likewise when there are incidences of sexual harassment at work, IBEC advises employers not to underestimate the damage, tensions and conflict which can ensue, coupled with a drop in productivity and efficiency.

Poor Customer Service

The growth of the service industry in Ireland, and the high degree of competition which this has generated, requires organisations to place a great deal of emphasis on establishing a quality service for customers. Whether it be a sales assistant in a supermarket, a cashier in a bank, a mechanic in a garage, or a waiter in a restaurant, the employee is the firm's representative when it comes to meeting customer needs. In the United States much research has been done into the link between employee attitudes and job satisfaction, and customer satisfaction. At Ford Motor Credit Company, it was found that attitudes regarding workload/stress, training/development, job/company satisfaction, and teamwork were all significantly related to customer satisfaction. (Johnson, Ryan, and Schmit, 1994) A positive correlation has also been found between employees who report high levels of satisfaction and their belief that they can deliver a quality service. (Schlesinger and Zornitsky, 1991)

A working environment where employees feel valued, are given sufficient training, and have a high level of job satisfaction facilitates a higher quality of customer service. (Schneider and Bowen, 1992) The very strong message coming from such research is that organisations which rely on their employees to provide an excellent and professional service neglect their employees' welfare at their own peril.

Poor work performance
The Institute of Personnel and Development (IPD) advises organisations to treat any form of intimidating or bullying behaviour as serious, because it can lead to under performance at work. *(Key facts: harassment at work)* If ignored, incidents of harassment may lead to, and perpetuate, a working environment in which it is unpleasant to work. People cannot contribute their best under such adverse conditions. Team work may be seriously hampered when workers are afraid of being harassed, criticised, bullied or abused. Demoralisation is a predictable consequence of such behaviour on workers.

Harassment extracts a high price. Staff can be subject to fear, stress and anxiety, which can put great strains on personal and family life. Harassment can lead to a lack of commitment, low morale, poor performance, and a feeling of tension and hostility in the workplace. The IPD advises employers and personnel officers to carry out regular reviews, attitude questionnaires and specific surveys, to ensure that policies and procedures to combat harassment are appropriate and effective.

Tom Kitt, Minister for Trade, Labour and Consumer Affairs

(in a speech made at the 12th Annual EAP Conference on 24 September 1997) stated that an organisation which does not acknowledge or deal with organisational stress will be beset by problems of poor work performance, poor time-keeping, increased absenteeism and lower productivity.

Negative image of organisation generated
In an article in *Personnel Management* (Vol 24, No 10, 1992), the author predicted that in companies where staff moral is low, costs will rise, productivity will suffer, absenteeism and staff turnover will increase, the firm will find it difficult to attract new staff, and their image and reputation will be damaged which will mean a further loss in business.

To succeed in today's highly competitive world, businesses must make substantial investments in marketing, advertising, and general promotion. The company's profile in the outside world must be impeccable, distinctive, and attractive. After spending thousands, hundreds of thousands, or even millions of pounds on creating, maintaining and enhancing such an image, the last thing in the world any business needs is adverse publicity. Having your business splashed across the Irish tabloids in bold print, linked with a case of sexual harassment or bullying is not very flattering. Less dramatic, but just as damaging, is the girl who tells everyone she's ever known, in graphic detail, about the desperate treatment she's received as an employee of hotel X, of store Y, or of factory Z.

When people love their work, their eyes light up when they talk about it. They brag about the delicious subsidised meals in the canteen, they rave about the big Christmas bonuses, and they thank their lucky stars that their boss is so great to work with. Not so with the abused, the down-trodden and the frustrated, the stressed and the bullied. They tell you they hate their work. It's a living nightmare. But they plan someday to get the boss or the bully back. And in their own way perhaps they do, by sharing the truth of their experiences, and blotting the squeaky-clean image of their firm with ferocious rage and bitter tears.

Case Study: Ken, twenty-seven-year-old administrator
'I worked for a short period of time with a stationery firm. I'd only worked there a couple of weeks when one of the managers nudged me and asked what I thought of the receptionist. Before

I had time to say she was a relative, he proceeded to give me a run-down on what he'd like to do to her when he got her into bed, adding that it wouldn't be long now because her contract was up for renewal the following month. I was furious. I could hardly contain myself. I called him a sick pervert. I warned him not to so much as look at the girl or he'd have to deal with me. He said I'd pay for that, then walked off. Most of what went on in there was down-right degrading. When my relative's contract was not renewed I was openly hostile to management, and I knew it was high time to move on myself.

My next job was with a printing company. It was like a breath of fresh air to find myself working with decent human begins. An order was imminent for a substantial contract for stationery, which would have been in excess of a hundred-thousand pounds. My former employers were suggested, as the firm's traditional suppliers. I was incensed and recounted my first-hand experience of this firm. I gave them my honest opinion that they were headed for disaster with such management as I had encountered at the helm. As a result the order was given to another company. I was absolutely thrilled that such an unworthy company had been exposed.'

CHAPTER SIX

What an employer can do to prevent and/or tackle harassment

A boss drives. A leader leads.
A boss relies on authority. A leader relies on co-operation.
A boss says 'I'. A leader says 'We'.
A boss creates fear. A leader creates confidence.
A boss knows how. A leader shows how.
A boss creates resentment. A leader breeds enthusiasm.
A boss fixes blame. A leader fixes mistakes.
A boss makes work drudgery. A leader makes work interesting.
(*Anonymous*)

ADOPTING A LEAD MANAGEMENT APPROACH

Lead management is an approach to managing workers which seeks to achieve the highest quality work possible, while simultaneously developing a happy, fulfilled and highly-motivated work-force. This is the antithesis of the boss management approach, discussed earlier, which is based on the premise that workers must be forced to engage in productive work by using a system of reward and punishment, so that 'good', loyal workers are rewarded, while those who are judged to be inadequate or unco-operative are systematically singled-out and punished.

In essence, lead management acknowledges that each human being is motivated to satisfy basic psychological needs for belonging, power, freedom and fun. When workers feel respected, supported, appreciated, and when they are consulted about the impact which proposed changes in working conditions will have on their jobs, they are much more likely to produce high quality work. When they are treated as highly valued team members, and involved with management in drawing up realistic targets and deadlines, they may even begin to sing the praises of their employers. The expertise and talents of workers are acknowledged, and they are encouraged to enjoy themselves while working. Co-operation, and not high levels of staff rivalry, is the backbone of this type of firm. It is acknowledged that con-

flict is a healthy part of life, so the discussion of workers' grievances and concerns is openly and actively encouraged. Each
worker is viewed as playing a key role in the overall success of
the organisation.

The lead manager

It is the manager's responsibility to inspire, support and motivate the work-force. This type of manager must have strong
leadership and interpersonal skills. Honest communication is
the cornerstone of lead management. The manager will not simply tell the workers what to do, but is capable of showing them
how to complete a new task before requesting that they do it,
and then makes certain that any difficulties are discussed until
the workers feel confident. Staff reviews are organised at set
periods, as are team meetings, where individual and team goals
can be clarified, and any uncertainty or difficulties discussed.
Self-evaluation is always encouraged. Criticism is kept to a minimum, but when a problem arises the causes are thoroughly explored, and the individuals involved are genuinely helped to
find a satisfactory solution. Lead managers operate an open-
door policy where ideas for improving any area of work are always welcomed.

In the lead management model, each worker is a valuable in-
gredient in the overall strategy and development of the organisation. Management is therefore aware that it is vital to invest in
its staff, to help each person achieve his or her full potential.
Continuous training is advocated, including training at all levels
of management, in self-development, stress management, conflict resolution, as well as technical and professional training.
The importance of staff recruitment, development, and health
and welfare are central to the organisation's personnel policy.
As salary is acknowledged as being a major incentive to workers, this is always kept in line with industry standards. When
productivity is particularly high, a bonus scheme is often introduced.

Job satisfaction and motivation

There have been many influential studies conducted in the area
of human relations from the 1920s onwards, into what gives job
satisfaction and what factors help to motivate workers. A sample of these are briefly outlined below.

The Hawthorne studies, under the direction of professor

Elton Mayo, are considered to be a major landmark in human relations at work. Researched between 1924 and 1936, the primary
emphasis was on studying workers in terms of their social relationships at work. The most significant lessons gleaned from the
studies were (1) work is a social activity, where workers are part
of a group and not isolated individuals; (2) the need for group
membership and status within the group is very important to
workers' sense of well-being and job satisfaction; (3) informal
groups at work exercise a powerful influence – either positive or
negative – in the workplace; (4) managers and supervisors need
to be aware of workers' social needs and cater for them, if workers are to collaborate with the objectives of the organisation, in-
stead of working against them.

Abraham Maslow's studies into human motivation led him
to propose a theory based on a hierarchical model of needs. At
the bottom were placed physiological needs, the need for food,
sleep, and sex. Then came safety and security, followed by the
need for love, affection and status within the group. Next came
the need for self-respect, and for the respect of others. At the top
was placed the need for self-fulfilment. Maslow's theories have
provided a useful framework for discussion as to the variety of
needs which people experience at work, and the ways in which
workers' motivation can be understood and met by managers.

Michael Argyle explored current psychological studies into
human motivation and work in his book *The social psychology of
work*. High levels of job satisfaction and motivation are experienced when (1) payment is at least adequate and in line with
market rates; (2) workers feel they are being treated fairly; (3)
there is good, open communication between workers and management; (4) workers feel involved as part of a cohesive team; (5)
work is interesting, and workers are given an opportunity to be
creative and flexible; (6) workers feel competent and in control;
(7) workers feel they are achieving something, which fills their
need for self-esteem; (8) promotion prospects exist; (9) workers
are consulted when goals are being set; (10) there is commitment
and loyalty to the organisation.

Dr William Glasser, founder of the Institute for Reality
Therapy, has advocated lead management in both education
and in the workplace. According to Dr Glasser, each person is
basically self-motivated, and we are never fully controlled by an
external source. People work, not only to survive, but also because it gives us the opportunity to have our psychological

needs, especially our self-esteem and social needs, fulfilled. Organisations which are aware of the psychological make-up of human beings, and which seek to enhance the working experience of its work-force, will thrive and expand due to the high level of quality of its products or services.

Case Study: Jim, thirty-seven-year-old waiter, SIPTU shop steward.
'I've worked fifteen years for a hotel in the West of Ireland. The first five years were hell on earth. There was a manager there who treated his staff like dirt. I was really in the firing line because I was elected shop steward. It was the kind of place you'd be embarrassed to tell anyone you worked. The service was sloppy, and staff-management relations were war-like. Although the location was perfect, dissatisfied customers were making sure that their friends would never as much as set foot in the hotel lobby. It wasn't too difficult to see why the locals called us 'Faulty Towers'. Conditions were appalling. I felt outright hostility towards my manager. That's why we joined a union in the first place. We had more disputes, and more complaints from our members as to mistreatment, than we could cope with.

And then miraculously it all changed, almost overnight. The owners must have realised that they were doomed unless the entire management structure was overhauled. The abusive manager was advised to seek alternative employment, and a new manager was appointed. Immediately he set about repairing a lot of the damage. He constantly validated staff. He got to know every worker by name. He showed enthusiasm for negotiating with the unions on pay agreements and general conditions. Even the most hostile and suspicious worker was won over by him. What amazed me was the night when we unexpectedly got reservations from a bus-load of American tourists, and two of our kitchen staff were out sick at short notice, and we were badly stuck. Our manager went into the kitchen, rolled up his sleeves and started doing the washing-up.

This manager really cared about people. He'd go out of his way to visit a member of staff who was after having a baby, and to bring her a bouquet of flowers. Most of us used to boycott the Christmas party, but from the first year that the new manager joined, you'd want to be on death's door before you'd miss it. Training was made available to every level of staff, to update their skills and give them qualifications. Every person, from the porter to the cleaner, began to take great pride in their hotel. And the result was, of course, startling. We developed a great name for excellence, and for having a friendly and competent staff. We couldn't keep up with the numbers who sought reservations. My own role as waiter greatly improved because I'd a well-trained staff working with me. I developed a brilliant working relationship with my manager. The level of staff complaints dropped dramatically, and relations between management and union became constructive and amicable.'

Lead management in action:
Andrew Rea, Projects Manager with G. C. McKeowns, Computer Software Consultants, Marshalsea Court, 23 Merchants Quay, Dublin 8.

'I have worked with McKeowns on and off for nine years. I started as a trainee programmer and have moved up the ranks to my current position. There are over one-hundred and sixty employees in the company, with about fifty-five of these working in the Dublin office where I'm based. We deal mainly with English clients in a support and development role. I have been in the role of Projects Manager for nearly three years now. I feel that management is a definite skill, one that requires on-going training, dedication, good communication skills and, most of all, good people skills.

Training: As stated earlier, I have followed the traditional route for middle management in Ireland by being promoted up the ranks, and was in the position of project leader for several years before being promoted to my present position. I have been on various training courses over this period, which dealt with project and human resources management. The area of human resource management is one that I have always had an interest in. I am a firm believer that, in this age of technology, people in an organisation are often the one resource which gives a company that cutting edge over competitors.

I have studied the Foundation Certificate in Professional Management with the College of Management Studies in Dame Street. On this course we covered the more traditional theories on managing people, such as Maslow's hierarchy of needs, and how these concepts could be applied to the workplace. These theories were interesting and did stimulate some thought. However, I learned that you cannot regiment the day to day management of human beings to a particular formula. In order to manage effectively, you must be flexible and willing to adapt to ever changing situations. After all, people are not clinical or predictable, especially in the workplace. Each person who I work with is unique, and what works effectively with one person may be disastrous with another.

I have really come to appreciate the importance of having someone to talk issues over with. I often discuss problems that I encounter with my own manager, my peers, and have been known to bend a friend's ear from time to time. This enables me to get another perspective on any difficult situation I encounter, especially those in which I am emotionally involved. This gives me a strong support network on which I can depend.

Communication: Communication is central to management and lack of it can cause a complete breakdown in a project team. From simply giving instructions, to building a relationship with the team members, it is probably the most important skill a manager needs. I try to keep a good level of communication between my staff and myself, also ensuring that it is a two-way process. Like any relationship, if I don't communicate misinterpretations can develop and the relationship will deteriorate. I feel it is important to get on well with the people I am working with, and to try to keep an interest in their lives in general. I always try to have a casual word with every one on the team and nurture a friendly and open relationship. I always keep my door open to the team members so that they can come to talk to me about problems, and I always make the time available to help them solve the issues raised. This applies to both work-related issues and to personal issues. We are all human and if something is upsetting a person then their work will obviously be affected, so it is in my best interest to help in any way I can. As a company we will try to accommodate any situations that arise, such as giving compassionate leave if required, or reducing the work load if necessary.

Responsibility: As a manager I have two responsibilities. The first is to the company, to ensure that the quality and quantity of work is produced in order to meet our targets. The second is to the people on my team. This responsibility ranges from ensuring their health and safety to ensuring that they have a rewarding and fulfilling working life. As with most things in life it is important that these two responsibilities are balanced and given equal importance, otherwise both will probably not be realised in the end. I aim to utilise and nurture each person's talents and apply them to the tasks we are required to carry out. I assume that people want to work and perform well in their job until I see signs that indicate otherwise. If this happens then I will investigate the situation and take the necessary steps to remedy any problems. Incentives are in place to help motivate the team, such as bonus schemes. However, I am careful not to fall in to the trap where you assume that money is the only motivater.

Motivation: One motivated person is worth at least three unmotivated people. A motivated person will not require close supervision, will be productive and will have a positive attitude to work. As a manager these are most desirable qualities in my team members. I try to motivate my staff in an all-encompassing manner. By this, I mean that I try to develop their careers, help them to feel fulfilled and happy in their work, and also that they are sufficiently rewarded for the work they carry out. I believe that people can get a lot of self-esteem from their work, that it is important that they feel good about their job, and that they gain recognition for their achievements. I will try not to criticise in a negative manner, and will always work in a positive way to help people overcome any problems or barriers that may exist. This is a very individualistic area, where different people are motivated by different things. As people develop, their needs change, and therefore what motivates them changes. This is one area where scientific theories fall down as they do not account for changes in a person's lifestyle or situation.

Recruitment: This is probably one of the hardest tasks that I carry out. The company puts a lot of time, money and effort into the recruitment process. Often people are technically trained in the areas but they may not enjoy the work proposed. I need to know that a person will really enjoy the position they are applying for, and that the investment made by the company will result in a long term relationship. I get great satisfaction from my job, and thus will apply myself to the best of my ability. I want to be surrounded by a team of people who are like minded and feel enthusiastic about the work they do. We use aptitude tests and interviews to select our staff, and when someone is employed we put them on six months' probation. This period is used to assess the person and to ensure that they can meet the required standards. Every support and encouragement possible is given, and the period is often extended in order to allow for different speeds of development. If at the end of this period we are not happy, then we will terminate the person's employment as we feel there is no benefit for either party working in an environment where both feel they are under-achieving.

Reviews: We hold annual performance and financial reviews as a norm. However, if at any time a manager or staff member seeks a performance review during this period it can be requested. The performance reviews are a very important process and one that I apply a considerable amount of time to. The performance monitoring is an on-going process which takes place during the review period. This information is then used at the review to discuss and measure the employee's performance. We have a defined procedure for carrying out performance reviews which involves both the manager and employee filling out a form which grades certain skills and competencies that are relevant to the position being reviewed. These forms are then used as part of the review, and are discussed and agreed. It is important that the staff member understands the process and is comfortable with it. It is a two-way process where credit is given if deserved, and positive criticism if required. As a manager I must be open to criticism myself as I am not perfect and can always improve on how I perform. Performance reviews can be a great motivater for employees. In our case, because our salary increments are linked with performance, it is even more important that they are carried out professionally.

Dealing with conflict: I like to feel I respect my staff and that they respect me. I will always ask that a task be carried out, and not order it. If a person is being unco-operative or obstinate, then I try to explore the cause of the problem, and not bring in an iron fist. Handling conflict in a constructive way requires a fair deal of skill and training. Exploring the problem with those involved, and seeking a solution where no one's self-esteem is damaged is tricky, but vital, for maintaining good staff relations. It can be important to be positive and unemotional when approaching the problem with the people involved to avoid heated situations. If a person is not performing to the required standards on a particular task then I always try to separate the actual task from the person. This means that performance of the task was not up to scratch, and not the person carrying out the task.

It is important also for the manager not to be seen as weak by avoiding conflict or by being inconsistent or undependable. As a manager I am a leader and role model to the people reporting to me, and I must keep this in mind always. If I expect my staff to stick to certain rules, say time keeping, then I must also adhere to the same rules. I am very conscious of managing by example.

Discipline: I am fully aware of the disciplinary procedures and the grievance procedures which are in operation in my company, as are the team members. Thankfully I have never had to use them. If a situation developed to the extent that I had to employ these procedure then they would be followed exactly. Usually, when a problem arises I discuss this with the person involved and clearly outline the issues. The discussion would focus on finding a solution and not harping on about the issue itself. Again, it is important that I have an open and honest relationship with staff so that both of us feel safe in this situation. If the discussion does not have the desired results then I would repeat the process. If I discovered that there was no improvement in the situation at that stage then I would utilise the procedures available. This is not a very nice part of management, but it is important that all of us follow the same rules, as anything else is unfair. I have a duty to the company and to the other team members to ensure that basic standards of discipline are maintained.

Generally we do not have a problem with discipline on our team as we have an open and frank communications network. We also hold regular meetings where grievances can be aired without having to go to formal procedures. If people are not satisfied with my response to their grievance then I would expect them to use the procedures available to them. I fully realise that I am not a perfect manager, and improvements can be made in how I perform. The only way I can discover my own weaknesses and strengths is by receiving and reviewing feedback from the people I manage. Therefore I welcome feedback.

Fairness: I try to be as fair and impartial as is humanly possible, and I avoid showing favouritism at all costs. Naturally everyone has personal likes and dislikes, but it is imperative that favouritism and discrimination are kept well out of the workplace. This can be very difficult as often members of staff will view situations from a very different angle than yourself, and whereas you think you are being fair and even-handed, they may feel victimised and discriminated against. Again keeping an open line of communication between the team and myself is my way of combating this problem. People can always approach me and let me know how they feel, and how decisions are effecting them. It is also important for me to realise that I may not be automatically incorrect in these situations, and that there may be external influences that are actually causing the employee's grievance.

I am loyal to my company and to my staff, but neither is based on blind loyalty. If there is something proposed by top management which will adversely effect my staff, then I will do everything in my power to persuade them to come up with an alternative or a compromise. Likewise, if a company objective needs to be met then I will also do everything in my power to help the team achieve it. In general if you treat the people on your team as intelligent human beings, and with basic respect, then they will develop a positive feeling towards the firm. Thus they will become more productive and happier members of staff.

Power and harassment: Handling power is not a problem for me. I don't need to have power over anyone, because as far as I'm concerned every person is a human being and deserves the same treatment that I would expect for my self. I may be a manager of a team project but that does not give me the right to mistreat any person involved in the project. It is company suicide to allow bullying or harassment to get a foothold, as each worker is a valuable resource to the company. I have done a lot of personal work on myself, and at this stage I have a good idea of my strengths and weaknesses. Needing to feel good by demeaning another human being is certainly not one of my failings.

Abuse of power and harassment is detrimental to any human relationship, and is a killer to the whole spirit of the workplace. Sure, I feel angry and frustrated sometimes, but these moods and feelings are never allowed to interfere with my professional approach to work. Whenever I feel angry I just take a few minutes to calm myself down, before tackling the situation. One burst of misplaced anger or frustration could ruin any trust which has been built up over years with team members.'

ESTABLISHING POLICY AND PROCEDURES FOR COMBATING HARASSMENT

Whether harassment at work is inflicted by a manager, supervisor, colleague, or a member of the public, ultimately it is the responsibility of the organisation to establish and maintain a policy of an harassment-free workplace. Where an employer fails to establish such a policy, and a case is taken by an employee against the firm, the employer could be held liable. The following preventative measures are recommended by the Employment Equality Agency to be implemented by all employers:

* Policies should be drawn up, expressing the employer's commitment to providing a working environment free of sexual harassment and bullying. These policies are most effective

when the chief executive is committed to their implementation and ensures that management and supervisors are informed as to their duties under it, and are adequately trained to carry out those duties
* Policies may be developed in consultation with employees' union representatives
* Both policies should then be issued in writing to all staff and managers, and then periodically circulated. New recruits should also be given a copy.
* Definitions of behaviours which constitute sexual harassment and bullying should be included in the policy. A person should be designated to handle sexual or other harassment complaints, and should be given appropriate training. Policies should also outline procedures to be adhered to if the problem does arise
* Training on sexual harassment and bullying should be part of the firm's general training programme for all employees.

A written policy should state that:
* All workers have a right to a work environment which is free from sexual harassment, and bullying
* Sexual harassment and bullying will not be condoned
* A named member of staff has been designated to handle complaints of sexual harassment and bullying
* Procedures for dealing with complaints will be made known to all employees
* Complaints will be dealt with seriously, quickly and confidentially
* A person who makes a complaint, or anyone who helps in the investigation of that complaint, will be protected from victimisation and retaliation
* Appropriate disciplinary measures will be taken if the complaint is proven.

INTRODUCING SAFEGUARDS AGAINST STRESS AND VIOLENCE

All places of work must have a safety programme written down in their safety statement. Employers need to safeguard the health and safety of workers from the effects of excessive levels of stress at work. They need to follow the safety procedures as advised by the Health and Safety Authority (*Workplace stress: Cause, effect, control*):
* Identification of potential problems

* An assessment of risks
* Implementation of safeguards
* Monitoring the effectiveness of the safeguards.

The traditional approach of management to stress was to train individual workers to cope. In practice it has been shown that any programme which concentrates solely on the worker is likely to be ineffective. Safeguards and controls must be implemented primarily at organisational level, i.e. at the source of the problem. This may mean changes in organisation, working conditions, social support, career development and training, management support, staff communication, and control of one's own work. These changes may then need to be supported by a programme of individual copying strategies.

Safeguards to help protect workers from the risk of violence should be implemented once the employer has identified that there is a potential risk. According to the Health and Safety Authority, these safeguards should be put in place as follows:
* Screens and partitions to improve protection from physical assault, and the exclusion of the public by using coded door locks and secure refuges for staff
* The installation of video surveillance and personal panic alarms and other emergency communications equipment which can deter the attacker
* Changing the layout of public waiting rooms, improving lighting and providing reading material
* Interview rooms should have an exit behind the staff member and a desk between employer and client. Glass panels should allow visual access of the staff member to other employees
* Cash free systems should be introduced, i.e. cheques, credit cards, tokens, etc. Time-locked sates should also be introduced where cash is handled
* Appropriate information should be provided for those waiting for attention. (*Violence at work*)

Training should be given to all staff in the recognition and avoidance of violent situations. Techniques of distraction and empathy, as well as break-away techniques and training in physical restraint can also be used. Conflict resolution and non-confrontational styles of approach can be taught to staff, to help prevent or diffuse potentially violent situations.

If violence does occur, treatment facilities, such as first aid and emergency support arrangements must be available. Support and counselling, either informally from a colleague who is trained in counselling techniques, or from a professional counsellor, should be provided if required.

ESTABLISHING GOOD INDUSTRIAL RELATIONS

Whether a full union structure is present in an organisation, or whether one or more workers are members of a union, it is important for management to promote a positive approach to industrial relations. In Ireland, industrial relations involves the employer and his or her representatives (management), workers and their representatives (the union), and the government. Unions seek to agree on a set of policies and procedures with management which will insure satisfactory wages and working conditions for workers, as well as protection against discrimination, victimisation and unfair or unreasonable job loss. Management can be aided by the setting-up of an effective union mechanism, enabling them to communicate with staff, to deal with conflict, and to give workers a forum to air grievances, to make suggestions and to offer ideas. The government is responsible for enacting legislation and staffing industrial relations institutions: the Labour Court, the Labour Relations Commission, and the Employment Appeals Tribunal.

Workers tend generally to feel more content knowing that they have union representation. This is particularly the case when workers are employed by large organisations which are financially and politically powerful. Employees need to feel that someone is looking after their interests. Unions have representatives at shop-floor, branch, and national level. The employer or human resources manager can benefit greatly from working closely with shop stewards, informing them of any pending changes in work practices, and consulting them where possible before any action is taken. As part of a company policy to maintain good employment practices, a joint company and union policy regarding bullying and sexual harassment may be issued to all staff, reassuring them that allegations of harassment will be investigated effectively and appropriately.

TRAINING FOR MANAGERS IN HUMAN RELATIONS AND RELATED AREAS

In July, 1987, the Minister for Labour established an advisory commission on management training in Ireland. A survey was done of the top 1,000 companies in the country. The findings of the commission showed a serious lack of management training throughout the public and private sectors. Over one-fifth of companies spent nothing on management training; over one half sent less than £5,000 per annum; foreign-owned companies spent 50% more than Irish-owned firms on management training and development. This was in stark contrast to industrial giants, such as the USA, which in 1985 spent an estimated 60 billion dollars on all forms of management development.

It was also found that Irish management courses tended to concentrate on certain areas, such as finance, accountancy, and business-environment subjects, and put little emphasis on marketing, human resources management and entrepreneurial development. The report gave guidelines on developing management skills, using informal systematic feedback on performance by senior managers, coaching and mentoring, personal counselling and career planning. (The advisory committee on management training, 1988)

Various studies (Gunnigle, Flood, Morley and Turner, 1988, 1990) comparing Irish companies with their counterparts in England, Northern Ireland and Scotland, revealed that Irish companies were less competitive in terms of labour, price, and the quality of skills. Inadequate training was identified as the major cause of these problems.

In 1995 Forfás produced a report of the extent and duration of management training in Ireland in a particular month (February 1994). Results revealed that just 11% of management had received training and that the duration was 1.8 days. A report of the incidence of labour-force training in the European Union, in the four week period preceding the survey (1992), revealed that only 7.1% of Irish workers had received training, compared with 24.3% in the Netherlands, 23.6% in Denmark, 18.3% in the UK, and 10.1% in Germany. (OECD, 1995)

In May 1997 a white paper on human resources development was published by the Department for Enterprise and Employment. The paper identified a serious lack of skills in Irish management, in particular team-working, team-leading, and customer/staff relations. The skills gap was the result of weak management entry-level skills, poor in-house training, deficiency in continuing training programmes, and in the structure and delivery of training received. For Irish companies to successfully compete with EU partners, the paper suggested that changes in traditional management/employee relationships would need to be implemented. These included the fostering of a more participative role for employees, which would promote greater employee interest in the overall success of the company, and more autonomy for staff in the performance of their jobs.

Developing a policy of training for managers and supervisors in the theories and practice of human relations management is a definite step which firms can take to become more competitive and to encourage and promote better employee-management relations. Training in basic communication skills, conflict resolution, assertiveness skills, and stress management will help managers to feel more confident in carrying out their managerial functions. This will at least go some way towards equipping managers with the correct tools to lead, motivate, delegate, and negotiate with individual employees and workgroups. Training in people skills will also highlight the importance of maintaining open, clear, and honest communication with staff at all levels.

A member of the human resources department may also be selected to train in basic counselling skills. This may be of great benefit when a staff member experiences personal difficulties such as bereavement, addiction, or relationship problems. In the case of serious or long-standing problems, a referral may be made to a professional counsellor. Counselling may also be helpful to staff who are having work-related problems. However, this service would need to be strictly confidential, and attended purely on a voluntary basis. The only exception to this would be if a member of staff was behaving in such an abusive or disruptive manner at work that counselling or rehabilitation was obligatory, as part of the firm's disciplinary procedures.

CHAPTER SEVEN

Support for employees:
What an employee can do in a case of harassment

Employees' reticence in reporting bullying and sexual harassment
Employees are reticent in reporting bullying and sexual harassment for a variety of reasons. Frequently victims feel frightened and anxious. After months or years of suffering verbal abuse, repeated criticism, or sexual innuendo, an employee usually feels powerless and inadequate. Victims may have been so badly intimidated that their self-esteem is very low, and they lack assertiveness. Many victims find themselves isolated, without any peer support. Their colleagues may have been so frightened themselves that they colluded with the bully, desperately trying not to be the target of the next attack. When the victim of harassment is male, he may fear losing face among colleagues for reporting incidences of abuse.

It takes great courage to come forward and to make a complaint. Often there exists a power-imbalance, in terms of status in the organisation, and the victim is of lower rank or grade than the harasser. Many employees lack knowledge of employment legislation. They may not be aware of what constitutes bullying or sexual harassment, or even how to go about making a formal complaint, unless they are in a union, or a policy outlawing harassment exists in their place of employment.

The greatest fear is that even if the person does make a complaint the harassment may not be dealt with fairly or adequately, and that the work situation might become even more intolerable. A multitude of questions can haunt the victim.
'He's so well in with the boss, how can I be sure of getting a fair hearing?'
'What if she remains in the department, I'll really be in for it then?'
'Could I be demoted?'
'Will I be branded a trouble-maker? Then I'll really be watched, and life won't be worth living.'
'What if no one believes me?'
'Maybe I'll be dismissed or forced out of my job?'

Aileen was in such a predicament. She was bullied and verbally abused by her boss for over five years. Asked why she never confronted the boss, she replied as follows:

'I tended to blame myself. I started thinking I must be a very stupid person. He must have known I was vulnerable. Most of the time I felt black despair. I had no support where I worked. The main reason I didn't do anything was the fear I had of losing my job, and of losing my home. I was frightened he'd say it was all my fault, that I was careless and inefficient. You'd have to at least have a proper personnel department who you'd know would be impartial before you'd report anything. But I didn't have that. There was no forum for airing grievances. The embarrassment was worse than anything else. I worked so hard, but it was all to no avail. He used to egg on the others to laugh at me. I thought there was something wrong with me. He used to call me paranoid. He told the others I was mad. I didn't know what bullying was. I had no label to say 'this is what's happening to me'. I just looked down at the desk when he'd shout at me. I'd go scarlet, but I'd never say anything. I thought it was my unlucky lot in life. Some women have a husband who beats them or a cruel boyfriend. I had an evil sadistic boss. I was so afraid he'd destroy my name and my character if I told anyone the horrible things he said. I felt so alone.'

It is absolutely crucial that victims of all forms of harassment are made fully aware of the support which is available to them. The Employment Equality Agency, under the Department of Justice, Equality and Law Reform, trade unions, and employer confederations, are all committed to eradicating harassment from the workplace, and to fully supporting the victims of any kind of abuse which they may be subjected to at work. Their central message to all victims is that no one has to remain silent, that there are organisations which are in place, to aid and support employees, in making a complaint, and in processing that complaint. Above all victims need never blame themselves. The blame rests, legally and morally, with the perpetrators.

What employees can do to help themselves
If you become aware that you are a victim of unwanted sexual attention, or are being bullied at work, then the following can be done to help your own case if the harassment continues, and you decide to make a complaint against the harasser:

* If you're not already in a union, then join one. This is your constitutional right, and even if you approach a union as an individual, you will be helped and supported by your nearest branch. If you fear further victimisation for joining a union, you need not tell anyone else in your workplace that you are a member, unless you need to bring in your union representative at a later date. This provides you with a source of support and advice on all employment issues. If you are already in a union talk to your shop steward or obtain direct advice from your nearest branch
* You may obtain advice and support directly from the Employment Equality Agency (EEA), on all issues relating to sexual harassment and inequality at work
* Log details of all incidences of harassment, including dates, times, and any witnesses who were present. Lodge these with your union official, the EEA or your solicitor
* Keep a copy of all memos sent and received relating to work
* Keep copies of work reviews and past references
* Canvass support from colleagues if this is at all possible, or at least confide in one colleague or friend as to what is happening at work
* Let your doctor know what is happening to you. If you are out on sick leave due to bullying or harassment, then it is a good idea for your doctor to put this on your cert.
* Contact a counsellor to help you deal with the emotions caused by the harassment, to help with self-esteem issues, and to explore if a similar situation has occurred in your past.
* Join an assertiveness group, or a stress management group, to help boost your own coping skills (see 'List of organisations and useful addresses' section).

Confronting the harasser informally
If you feel strong enough you may wish to confront the harasser informally, before making a formal complaint. It is always a good idea to have some kind of support in place before taking this approach however, as confrontation may lead to an escalation of the problem. You may confront the harasser by:
* Approaching the person directly, stating the behaviour which you find intimidating, degrading, or offensive, and requesting that this behaviour be stopped. Follow this up by sending a memo, stating your request, for the record
* If you do not want to take the direct approach, then you can

send a memo to the harasser, without speaking to the person directly
* You may wish to have a third party present, such as a friend, a colleague, or a supervisor. If you are a member of a union, you can ask your union representative to state your grievance to the person concerned, or you can do so yourself in the union representative's presence.

Making a formal complaint

If the above informal approach does not solve the problem, or if the harassment is of a serious nature, then you can bring a formal complaint against the harasser. If a policy exists in your workplace outlawing sexual harassment and bullying, you may make a complaint under the grievance procedures as outlined in the policy. Under this policy there should be a person designated to handle your complaint. Ideally, a person of the same sex should be made available if requested.

Both complainant and accused are encouraged to seek advice and representation at an early stage. If you are in a union your union representative can be present to support you in making a complaint, and during the investigation. If both yourself and the harasser are members of the same union, then you must have representation from two different union representatives. Whether or not a policy exists, you are entitled legally to make a complaint under the firm's grievance procedures. You can approach personnel or your manager to make a complaint. If your manager is the source of your complaint, then you can contact a more senior manager.

The investigation

Your complaint should be investigated confidentially if at all possible, and with the minimum of delay. Both parties will be interviewed before a judgement is given. Having a log of incidences that occurred over a period of time will be invaluable when the investigation proceeds. Also, if there are any witnesses who are prepared to come forward and to state what they saw or heard, or to verify the effects which the bullying or sexual harassment has had on you, then this will be most helpful to your case. It may be difficult to keep calm, and not to verbally attack the person who has been harassing you, but it will be more helpful to stick to the facts when being interviewed, and to be well prepared.

The investigator will keep a record of all interviews and meetings held during the investigation. A range of penalties should be previously stated, depending on the severity of the harassment. If the investigation concludes that one of the parties should be transferred, you should not be transferred unless this is requested. Where a complaint is not upheld by the formal investigation, this does not necessarily indicate that the complaint was malicious. You have a right to appeal if you are dissatisfied with the decision of the investigation.

Taking legal action
A legal case can be brought against your employer in any of the following circumstances:
   * The harassment is of an extremely serious or criminal nature
   * You are dissatisfied with the investigation undertaken by your employer into your complaint, and wish to pursue the matter further
   * You are victimised for having made a formal complaint
   * You are unfairly dismissed
   * You are forced into leaving your employment due to the severity of the harassment.

STATE AGENCIES
The following agencies are available to give employees advice and support on employment legislation, and to provide professional representation.

The Employment Equality Agency (EEA).
The Employment Equality Agency was established under the Employment Equality Act (1977), by the Department of Justice, Equality and Law Reform. It's function is to help make the legislation work. It has a major role in promoting equality of opportunity and treatment between men and women at work. The EEA has the power to refer a case to the Equality Officer of the Labour Relations Commission where it believes discrimination is being practised, or where an employer is in breach of legislation. EEA provides a free confidential advisory service to employers, employees, trade unions and the legal profession on the operation of the employment equality legislation. It also offers assistance to those who experience unfair treatment at work. Where an issue does not come under equality legislation, it will refer people to other appropriate agencies.

EEA assistance has focused on certain priority areas in recent years, such as sexual harassment, pregnancy discrimination, the treatment of part-time and casual workers, and discrimination in promotion and in non-traditional areas of employment. At it's discretion, the EEA may carry out an investigation into the complaint, prepare and issue a letter of complaint to the party allegedly responsible for the discrimination, or refer a case to the Labour Court.

Case Study: Jennifer, thirty-six-year-old accounts assistant

'I'm employed by a large department store in the accounts section. I was on very good terms with both staff and management for the first three years, until a problem arose. The company decided to introduce a uniform for all female staff. The personnel officer sent us each a memo, advising that a uniform would be introduced the following month, and requesting that we each state the size of clothes required. I certainly didn't want to wear a uniform. A few girls in other departments were also against it, but they didn't want to rock the boat and refuse to wear it, in case they'd be labelled trouble-makers. My colleagues were all male, and so they were not required to wear a uniform. My own boss, who was female, was given a choice as to whether or not she wished to wear it.

On the advice of a friend I rang the Employment Equality Agency. I was informed that there was no legal requirement for me to wear a uniform, as I was not dealing with the public, and other staff at my own level were not wearing one. I informed personnel of the EEA's view on the uniform issue. Their response was to send me a memo, requesting that I attend a meeting with my manager. She reiterated the company's policy, and hinted that a dim view would be taken of my uncooperative attitude – particularly if I involved an outside body in internal matters. She suggested I have a rethink, to consider my career prospects and my future with the firm.

I was worried if what my manager said constituted a threat to my job, although dismissal was not directly mentioned. It was clear though that I'd be victimised in some way if I didn't conform. If I hadn't felt so strongly about uniforms I'd probably have fallen in with the rule, because I certainly felt intimidated. But I was an adult, not a school girl, and I hated the idea of someone dictating to me what I should wear. And anyway, how could I expect to be taken seriously by my male colleagues if I had to dress in a tacky uniform while they had no such restrictions? I rang the EEA again, and made an appointment to meet with one of the equality officers. I conveyed the contents of the meeting to him, and he reassured me that I was within my rights, and could not be victimised in any way for refusing to wear the uniform. I gave him my permission to formally write to my company, advising them of equality legislation and its interpretation as regards the wearing of uniforms.

A week later I was requested to attend another meeting with my manager. She was somewhat agitated and semi-hostile. She informed me that I was exempt from wearing the uniform, but told me in no uncertain terms not to influence any other member of staff on this matter. My relationship with my manager was permanently damaged after this episode. She started scrutinising my work, checking up on my time-keeping and behaving in a vindictive manner towards me. I certainly feel she has it in for me. At the very least my working life has become uncomfortable. Everyone has commented on the change in the way I'm treated, so it's not just my imagination. Still, I don't regret invoking the Employment Equality Agency, because why should I have put up with unfair treatment when the law was on my side? I still feel better for having stood up for myself, and if I wish to make a fresh start elsewhere I can always do so.'

The Health and Safety Authority (HSA)

The Health and Safety Authority was set up under the Safety, Health and Welfare at Work Act, 1989, by the Department of Enterprise, Trade and Employment. The emphasis is on preventing accidents and ill-health from occurring by identifying workplace hazards, both physical and psychological, and putting appropriate safeguards in place. The HSA provides information and advice to employers and employees relating to prevention of accidents and ill-health. It is made up of representatives from workers, employers and the state. Health and safety inspectors monitor the observation of legislation at workplaces, and they have the authority to enforce measures up to and including prosecution.

INDUSTRIAL RELATIONS BODIES

The Labour Court

The Labour Court consists of employee's representatives, employer's representatives, and an independent chairperson. It's

functions include investigating disputes, issuing recommendations for their settlement, and deciding on appeals. Labour
Court hearings are informal. Hearings of the court are held in
private, unless one of the parties requests a public hearing. The
court can hear evidence under oath, summon witnesses and request to see relevant documents. There are no legal costs involved in bringing a case to the Labour Court.

You can take a case to the Labour Court yourself, but it is
strongly advised that you seek advice and assistance from a
trade union, or from the EEA. It should also be noted that in the
case of sexual harassment, there is a six months time limit from
the first occurrence of the alleged harassment within which you
must lodge your complaint.

The Labour Court issues legally binding determinations in
cases such as an appeal against a Right's Commissioners' or an
Equality Officers' recommendation. Otherwise recommendations are not legally binding on the parties. It can award compensation to a maximum of two years salary. Determinations
may be appealed to the High Court, and subsequently to the
Supreme Court, though most cases do not proceed beyond the
Labour court.

Equality Officers
When an employee is victimised for making a complaint, or for
giving evidence during an investigation, a victimisation complaint may be referred to an Equality Officer. Equality Officers
are attached to the Labour Relations Commission, and they investigate complaints under equality legislation. The Equality
Officer has wide power during an investigation and can, for example, visit the work premises, carry out a work inspection, request all documents connected with a complaint and interview
key individuals. Following the investigation, the Equality
Officer will issue a recommendation. This is not legally binding
on the parties. The recommendation may be appealed to the
Labour Court within 42 days of the date of issue.

Rights Commissioners
Rights Commissioners operate as a service of the Labour
Relations Commission. They are empowered by the Industrial
Relations Act (1969) to investigate certain industrial disputes.
They deal mainly with disputes involving individual workers.
A Right's Commissioner, however, cannot carry out an investi-

gation unless both parties, i.e. the employee and the employer, are in agreement. Having carried out an investigation, the Right's Commissioner will issue a recommendation which is not legally binding on either party. Either of the parties can appeal the recommendation to the Labour Court.

The Employment Appeals Tribunal

The Tribunal consists of a chair-person, twenty vice-chairpersons, and a panel of forty members, twenty nominated by the ICTU, and twenty nominated by employer's organisations. The Tribunal determines matters of dispute arising under the Redundancy Payments, Minimum Notice, Maternity Protection, Adoptive Leave, Unfair Dismissals, Protection of Employees, Worker Protection, Payment of Wages, Terms of Employment, and Protection of Young Persons Acts.

TAKING A CIVIL OR A CRIMINAL CASE

A person may take a civil or criminal action against an employer for harassment. In this case legal advice may be obtained from a solicitor. The advantage of taking such a case is that compensation for injury incurred is usually much greater than the Labour Court will award. Unless free legal aid is available however, or a union is prepared to take a civil case on behalf of a member, there is always the danger of losing the case and of having to pay both your own and your employer's legal fees, which can be extremely costly.

ORGANISATIONS WHICH OFFER ADVICE AND SUPPORT

Advice, and support on fair procedures and employment legislation, and professional representation is available from state agencies (outlined above), and from trade unions. Emotional support is available from voluntary organisations which specialise in working with victims of harassment, and from professional counsellors and psychotherapists.

Trade Unions

Irish Congress of Trade Unions (ICTU)

The ICTU is the central authority for the trade union movement in Ireland. (See Trade Unions in 'Useful Addresses', for list of individual unions.) There are 68 unions affiliated to the Congress, some of which operate in Northern Ireland. Membership of affiliated unions is in excess of 680,000, with membership in the Republic of Ireland representing two thirds of that total. The main function of the ICTU is to co-ordinate the work of trade unions, and to represent the interests of members on government advisory bodies: the Labour Relations Commission, and the Labour Court. Its education and training service provides a comprehensive trade union education programme for shop-stewards, officials and members of affiliated unions.

Tom Wall is Assistant General Secretary of ICTU, and a member of the Health and Safety Authority. His own specialisation is industrial relations.

'There is an agreed approach to combating bullying and harassment in employment between all unions. We urge employers to set down a policy, combating bullying and harassment in the workplace. This is issued jointly, by employer and union, to all employees. The agreement should permit a confidential system of initiating complaints, independent expert intervention, and counselling for individuals. It should stipulate the grievance and disciplinary procedures which will be used, and should emphasise that the person who has been bullied is not the person who will be penalised.

In firms where a union is in place an employee can make a complaint to the shop steward, or to the health and safety representative, without having to go directly to management. The shop steward could then be present during the investigation, if that's what the person wants. There is an in-built advantage for all concerned if there is a union. We train union reps, and health and safety reps, in how to deal with complaints, and how to initiate discussions with employers as to the implementation of the policy and procedures. We always recommend that a well-qualified, independent person is involved in any investigation following a complaint. Some organisations have employee assistant programmes in place, which can be very supportive for the individual concerned.

Support is very important. In our booklet 'Bullying in the workplace: Guidelines for action', we define the most common form of bullying – non-physical, as 'persistent psychological violence.' This is most common where the person has no peer support. Physical aggression and assault are criminal offences and can be dealt with by contacting the authorities. When we first launched the booklet, we had a lot of calls from victims of bullying, looking for support.

In the case of an individual who has joined a union, and who makes a complaint of harassment, it's not as clear-cut. Some organisations won't recognise the right of a union to represent a worker. That's the crux with the union recognition issue. Employees need expert support. If they can't have a union official present they are entitled to have their solicitor, but the solicitor will require remuneration for time and services, and that could be very costly.

If a person is not happy with the outcome of the investigation, then there are alternative routes. Sexual harassment is covered under the Employment Equality '77 act. The Safety, Health and Welfare '89 act, doesn't sufficiently protect the worker from bullying. There's no proper legislation in place to do that. To my knowledge no one has taken a case under the '89 act. Under the unfair dismissals act, a person is entitled to take a case against an employer where bullying has been perpetrated. The Employment Appeals Tribunal deals with dismissal cases. So if conditions are so damaging that a person can't work under them, then constructive dismissal may be the best way to proceed. The maximum compensation under any of these acts is two year's salary. That's why civil cases may become more popular, because damages awarded may be much higher.'

The role of trade unions in combating harassment

The ICTU has issued very clear guidelines to all union officials and representatives as to their responsibilities in striving to ensure a working environment which is free from bullying and sexual harassment:

* Unions should highlight the problem in magazines and newsletters and through discussions at union meetings
* Bullying, sexual harassment, and how to deal with them should be included on training courses for officials and union representatives
* Members should be informed of their rights and their duty to report incidences of bullying and harassment
* Unions should, during negotiations, raise the issue of bullying and sexual harassment, and the need for workplace awareness of the problem
* A model agreement should be developed and implemented
* Bullying, intimidation or sexual harassment at union meetings or in connection with any representative function should never be tolerated.

As the majority of victims of sexual harassment are women, male union officials and representatives need to be aware of, and sensitive to, the nature and scope of the problem. They are expected to respond to complaints in a supportive way. Representation of a member should be by a person of the same sex if requested. Where both the complainant and the alleged harasser are represented by the same union, both representatives are to be at the same level in the union. Officials and representatives are expected to set acceptable standards of behaviour by their own example.

Unions as a source of professional support for employees
SIPTU Branch Secretary, Frank O'Malley, of the Hotels, Restaurants and Catering Division at Liberty Hall, Dublin, highlights the advantages of joining a union for workers in all sectors of employment.

There are people out there who believe there's no need to join a union. There are even those who would go so far as to say that unions are anti-work, and that union officials are nothing more than a crowd of communists and conspirators. Unions are often grossly misrepresented, particularly by employers. Unions are blamed for everything: if there's a strike, it's the unions fault; if a firm closes down, it's the union again. But when we look at the facts, the number of gains which Irish workers have made as a result of trade union lobbying, such as greater holiday entitlements and sick-pay, we begin to get a more realistic picture. Workers have better working conditions, not because employers have willingly introduced them, but because trade unions have represented worker's interests, politically as well as at organisational level.

The union has built-in safeguards to ensure that high standards of professional conduct are maintained by officials. If for any reason a member has a grievance to make against a union official or a representative this can be made through the union's complaint's procedures. Complaints can be made at regional or national executive level. Unions are also maligned for representing members who are charged with perpetrating bullying or harassment. It can happen that both alleged victim and bully are members of the same union. Quite simply every person has a right to be represented, and as a professional organisation, SIPTU must ensure fair and equitable treatment for all members. However, SIPTU does not in any way condone abusive behaviour, and those found guilty of such behaviour must be dealt with under the firm's disciplinary procedures.

There are many advantages to workers, either as individuals who wish to join a union, or as groups who seek to organise a union structure in their workplace. Unions offer professional advice, and professional representation to their members. Usually the union official will know more about the law and correct procedures than the employer, so that's a decided advantage for the worker. SIPTU has a legal section, which includes qualified barristers, to give advice on any issues which may arise. A worker may be pushed to the point where a situation becomes unbearable, and has no choice but to leave. Workers in this predicament need professional representation. Also SIPTU has divisions which represent every sector of industry: electrical, catering, hospitals, finance, etc. So workers are usually represented by people who have themselves worked in the same industry. How many workers could afford to approach a solicitor for that kind of representation? The full service, all that support and advice, is available to every member, right around the country, for £2-something a week.

Workers who are being bullied or harassed especially need this kind of support and advice. I would advise anyone who is experiencing discriminatory or bullying treatment to chronicle even the smallest issues that arise, such as the day, date, and time of every incident that occurs. You've then got to lodge these documents with somebody, preferably a union official who you get to know and have confidence in. These will then be stamped by the union, so you have proof that over a period of time you documented these incidents. Often there won't be any witnesses, as most bullies do their harassing behind closed doors, so this will be your only way of collecting evidence. In this way you can gradually build a case until you have enough evidence to take on the employer.

I also like to give those who are being bullied some insight into the bullies' make-up. Bullies most often pick on people they know they can intimidate. Bullies want their victims to cry and break-down in front of them. That's where they get their buzz from, the feeling of being in control. If a worker who's being bullied could just sit there with a smile on her face while the bully shouts and screams, waits until he's finished, and then says 'let me write down all that you've just said.' I've seen that work before. It really phased the bully, and ruined his power-trip.

When you prepare to take a case to law you're not simply talking about what is morally correct. You have to ensure that you are legally correct. People often think that unions should resolve every issue, but there are cases that we cannot resolve, in the same way that solicitors can't guarantee to win every case. So in advising a member in how to proceed, we have to be very careful. We don't want the member to be damaged further, or to feel let-down. It's not only a question of what the truth is. Let's take the case of a man who is being bullied. He is at a distinct disadvantage – legally, because it's expected that a man should be able to fight his own corner. It would be much easier to take the same case, if it involved a female, and win it. 90% of cases of bullying I've dealt with have involved females. Only once have I come across a case where a man reported being bullied by a woman. The problem is, that it's all to do with how credible a case sounds. Then there are cases which could be too damaging for the worker involved if it went to court, no matter what the outcome. If the worker is from a family which has a very high profile, then the media publicity might cause too many problems. It simply mightn't be worth the personal distress involved to pursue the case.

There are many flaws in the law from the point of view of workers. For instance, I may take a case to the right's commissioner, but unless the employer agrees to proceed with the investigation, the commissioner won't intervene. Then there's the Labour Court. Recommendations are not legally binding, so an employer may give the ruling a two-finger sign. There's nothing I can do about that. The only tribunal that an employer has to attend, and abide by its decision, is the Employment Appeals Tribunal, in an unfair dismissal's case.

The law is based on protecting the rights of property and hence the moneyed-classes, much more than on protecting an individual's rights. This is something a person should be wary of if thinking of taking civil action. Unless there is overwhelming evidence that the employer is liable, it's very risky. There could be big legal costs involved if you employ a solicitor, and you don't win the case. There's another flaw with regard to the law and unions. An employee has a constitutional right to join a union, but the employer does not have to negotiate with the union.

There are some cases where you know that the relationship has so utterly broken down between worker and employer that the worker has to leave the employment. Then it becomes a matter of compensation, and we'll be aiming to reach a settlement with the employer. It's usually the fear of adverse publicity which will persuade the employer to pay compensation in such as case. The union is there to give advice on the various pitfalls which might arise in a particular case, and to give support when the member decides on an appropriate course of action.

Case Study: Emer, twenty-five-year-old retail assistant

'For months my employer had it in for me. It was a personal vendetta. He had a falling out with a member of my family, so he wanted to get even with me. He watched me day in and day out. I couldn't even blink without him knowing about it. He'd often say crude and nasty things to me when he got me alone. I tried for other jobs but I didn't get them. I had no knowledge of unions, except I knew my boss would go to any lengths to keep them out. I was really scared myself in case I'd join a union and they'd use me to get a foothold in the firm. There were four of us working in the shop, and I knew the others wouldn't have the guts to join. It was only when my employer threatened me with dismissal that I joined as a last resort.

I couldn't have been more wrong about the union. I went to my local branch and told Joe, the union official, the whole story. I was in tears most of the time. He was really sympathetic and understanding. He advised me to keep a record of any more incidences, and he promised to support me if I was dismissed. That was such a weight off my mind. I must have rang Joe several times every week after that. He'd always ring me back if he wasn't there at the time, and give me useful advice about what to do, or what to say, when I'd been wrongly accused of something by my bullying boss.

In the end I couldn't take it any more. I'd collected a whole note book of incidents and I asked Joe to come in and try to get me a redundancy package. I really needed to get out. It was a hard slog. Joe confronted him about his abusive treatment of me. I was amazed that I lost all fear when Joe was beside me. At long last I had the chance to tell my boss exactly what I thought of him. He was all nice and charming when Joe was there. Now it was his turn to be scared. Joe finally got me a good deal. Without his help I'd have left months before, with nothing.'

EMOTIONAL SUPPORT

Voluntary organisations

Anti-Bullying Centre (ABC).

Dr. Mona O'Moore is co-ordinator of the Anti-Bullying Centre (ABC), and senior lecturer in Child and Educational Psychology, in Trinity College. The ABC urges those who are, or who have been, victims of bullying at work to get help, to share their experiences, and to contribute to the research into bullying which is being conducted at the centre.

'My original research involved bullying in schools. As my roots are in Scandinavia, and much pioneering research into bullying at work has been conducted there, I became interested in investigating the extent of workplace bullying in Ireland. I was also asked to write several articles on bullying at work, and my name became linked to this area of research. I then developed the Anti-Bullying Centre for adults and children who were experiencing bullying. Since then there has been a lot of media attention generated, and as a result there has been a surge of people coming forward to report their experiences of workplace bullying.

I see the centre as having an independent voice. We have no funding, and we rely on voluntary contributions. At present there is just myself and two assistants running the centre. We offer people advise and information. We also draw up depositions for them which can be used if they decide to take a case to court. Referrals are sometimes made to the centre by solicitors and trade unions. We ask those who contact the centre to fill in a questionnaire. This provides us with empirical data for our research into the extent of workplace bullying in Ireland. We also have the services of three counsellors for individuals who need to work through their experiences. Some people are quite desperate when they call to us and they really need this service.

Clearly people see us as a National centre, as we get calls from people all over the country, and from all sectors of employment. I would like to set up regional support centres, which would be linked to the Dublin centre, and which would provide advice and counselling for anyone suffering from bullying in their place of work. I've also worked with various companies, such as the ESB, advising them on policy-making, and I'm on SIPTU's working party, which seeks to tackle all forms of bullying in the workplace. My aspiration for the centre is to receive sponsorship so we can employ a full-time counselling psychologist, and a researcher.

Bullying at work can have very serious consequences for those effected. 65% of those I saw in a one-month sample had suicidal tendencies. People can feel like an animal in a trap, with no way out. I've often spoken to people who are nervous wrecks because of the kind of treatment they've been subjected to. The personality of the person may change. All of this abuse is so totally unnecessary. The majority of the people who I have spoken to who have been bullied are not weak, incompetent or inadequate people. They are usually very competent people, who just happen to be in the wrong place at the wrong time. They may have been very happy in their work for seven, fifteen or twenty years. Then a new boss is appointed. He may not like the person, or he may feel insecure because the person has better qualifications than he has. The bullying may be verbal, psychological or physical, and may be repeated and systematic. In the majority of cases the victim is not inviting an attack: it's the bully who has the problem. People who have been victimised at work need to be made aware of what is happening to them, and to be given the support to confront it.

In Ireland and the UK, the structure of organisations tends to be hierarchical, which may have a bearing on the extent of bullying in these countries. Organisations need to recognise that their most important asset is their staff. Otherwise they will lose business. Motivation and team spirit depend on treating their staff well, with respect and dignity. Research shows that this is associated with high productivity. The 'survival of the fittest' ethos needs to be replaced by basic human Christian principles. Managers need to be trained to treat their staff well, and there's an onus on education to foster these basic principles in schools.

The week after my appearance on the 'Late Late Show' in November last, we received 270 calls from victims of bullying. Since the centre has opened we've received calls and letters from hundreds of people who have been bullied at work. When we have completed the research work at the centre we will be in a position to publish statistics on the extent of bullying in organisations throughout Ireland.'

Campaign Against Bullying (CAB)
Vivette O'Donnell of the Campaign Against Bullying, has actively combated bullying in schools and in the workplace since 1983. CAB offers advice, information, and consultations to anyone who is experiencing bullying. CAB has also been an impor-

tant pressure group, lobbying politicians and urging the Health and Safety Authority to put bullying at the top of its agenda. CAB receives calls from workers of all occupations and sectors. People are sometimes referred by the Employment Equality Agency when a case does not fall within their particular sphere. Seminars, workshops, and conferences are periodically run to increase public awareness on the whole issue of bullying.

In Vivette's experience, bullying occurs when there is a fundamental lack of respect, honesty and justice. Bullying causes victims to feel humiliated, to be falsely accused, to be undermined and devalued, to feel worthless, and to be depicted as deviant. When a workplace bully/bullying manager has been identified and found guilty, Vivette advises that disciplinary action should result in either '(1) dismissal, (2) suspension, (3) demotion, (4) probation with stricter regulations on work practices, and (5) rehabilitation and training. The bully should never be promoted, transferred to a similar position of authority, given immunity from discipline and rehabilitation, or depicted as the injured party. The bully must give acknowledgement of the injuries which he/she has caused to the victim, an apology, and an undertaking to reform.'

According to Vivette, 'Feelings of distress and powerlessness are greatly increased by lack of support from those applied to, e.g. higher management, union, colleagues, and personnel department. Lack of or sparse communication, slow processing of information, unfriendly communication multiply the effects of the bullying ... Speed and courtesy are of the essence. It generally takes at least a year for a victim of more than a month of bullying to recover and to heal to 98% of their former self. This fact also needs to be understood and acknowledged – the victim cannot heal unless the hurt and the slow recovery are both acknowledged with proper regret.'

Vivette emphasises the importance of having good management practices and procedures in the workplace, as an insurance against bullying. She advises employers to interview staff members before they leave, to ascertain the real reasons for their departure. CAB handles about 50 cases of workplace bullying each year, in addition to an unrecorded number of enquiries. About 80% of calls are from victims whose health has been injured as a result of workplace bullying. 10% come from personnel/human resources managers and trade union representatives/officials, 5% from bullies trying to justify their behaviour, and 5% from researchers. About 70% of these complaints are resolved in a relatively short space of time. However, some cases are still unresolved after several years of endeavour.

Rape Crisis Centre

The Rape Crisis Centre provides counselling for any person who has experienced sexual assault, rape or sexual harassment. It is a completely confidential service, where individuals are treated sensitively and helped to work through their feelings in a supportive environment. A lot of perpetrators of sexual harassment try to laugh it off and to claim that the woman was asking for it, to protest that their behaviour was just a harmless bit of fun, and to insist that what someone wants to pin up on their office wall is their own affair. The centre emphasises that to the victim of sexual harassment this kind of behaviour is certainly no joke, and is highly offensive and demeaning. It urges victims of sexual harassment at work not to suffer in silence but to come forward and to seek professional support.

Counselling and psychotherapy

Counselling provides an opportunity for individuals to explore the roots of any upsetting or traumatic experiences they may have had in the past, or which they are experiencing in the present. The counsellor offers support in a non-judgmental, caring and confidential environment. Counselling can help people to express and work through confusing or overwhelming emotions, such as sadness, anger, despair, hurt, and fear. Psychotherapy is similar to counselling, but tends to look deeper into past experiences and deep-seated issues, seeking to bring about change from old habits and patterns of behaviour.

The counsellor facilitates the growth of the person's self-understanding and self-esteem. Through counselling, individuals become more aware of the different options which are available to them, to help resolve their problem. Counsellors do not give advice, but encourage clients to make their own decisions. This is particularly helpful for those who have experienced, or who are experiencing, bullying or sexual harassment at work.

The effects of harassment in some cases are devastating, and are best resolved by seeking the support of a professional counsellor or psychotherapist. Those people who have perpetrated harassment at work on colleagues or subordinates, either deliberately or unwittingly, may also benefit greatly from undergoing psychotherapy. (A list of various counselling and psy-chotherapy organisations which make referrals to professional therapists is given in 'List of organisations and useful addresses' section).

CHAPTER EIGHT

Training and support for employers

DEALING WITH A COMPLAINT OF HARASSMENT

Complaints of harassment must be taken seriously, and dealt with promptly, and confidentially as far as possible. This is where it is a major advantage to have a policy combating harassment in place, and to have previously outlined a range of penalties for harassment, depending on the severity. Procedures for dealing with the harassment should be based on the principles of fairness and natural justice.

An investigation must be pursued with due respect for the rights of both the complainant and the alleged harasser. An investigator, who should be independent and impartial, will interview both parties and record details of all interviews and meetings held, with a view to establishing the truth. Representation by a union official or other person should be made available to both parties.

Examining the complainant's evidence

It is always a traumatic and difficult experience to make a complaint about a colleague or manager. Fear of not being believed, of not getting a fair hearing, and of being subjected to further victimisation, are all likely to be foremost on the complainant's mind during an investigation, especially if the alleged harasser holds an authoritative position in the firm. The complainant's story should therefore be listened to with sensitivity. In many cases of harassment there are no witnesses present, and establishing the truth boils down to which person's story you believe.

The investigation should take into account the complainant's track record with the firm, references from previous firms, whether or not there has been a sudden deterioration in work performance, records of absenteeism, and colleagues' confidential opinions on the work-place environment. It may be possible to ascertain if there are any motives which the complainant might have for wrongly accusing the person: Is there rivalry for promotion? Does the complainant appear to be envious of the accused?

Examining the accused's evidence
Bullies are adept at being able to charm and fool people into thinking that everything they are accused of is the other person's problem. He or she may have superior verbal skills, and may exude confidence. The complainant may be accused of:
   * under performing
   * making mistakes
   * having an attitude problem
   * being lazy and irresponsible
   * having a poor attendance and time-keeping record
   * being incompetent and failing to meet deadlines
   * having a grudge against the accused
   * being a trouble-maker
   * being paranoid.

Again, it is important to interview colleagues to ascertain if any of them are having problems with the accused, or with the complainant, as bullies usually cause problems for more than one member of staff. The accused's attitude to managing or team-working should be examined. Personality traits should be analysed: How does this person handle pressure? Does he/she need to be in control? Is this person full of anger, aggression and hostility? Does he/she isolate or show favouritism towards certain staff members? Does this person have a compulsion to criticise and humiliate others but rarely to give praise? Is a personal vendetta being carried out against the complainant?

Making a decision
The investigator must make a decision and relay this to both parties. Penalties for harassment may range from a reprimand, to transfer and demotion, to dismissal. Penalties should be imposed for victimisation of either the complainant or a witness. An appeal mechanism must be available for both parties, for the alleged victim if it is concluded that sexual harassment or bullying has not taken place, and for the alleged harasser if the complaint is upheld.

   The workplace should be carefully monitored following a complaint which is held to be well-founded. Employee reviews should be introduced if not already in place, and confidential surveys should be periodically carried out. In particular the offender should be closely supervised, and all precautions taken to prevent further harassment or victimisation being taken against the complainant.

Employee Assistance Programmes

Counselling should be made available to the victim, if requested. A rehabilitation program, including psychotherapy, may be made compulsory for an employee found guilty of harassment. Employee Assistance Programmes (EAP) may be offered by firms. This is a confidential counselling service, available free of charge to employees. The employer is provided with regular reports from the EAP, containing statistical information and indicating the nature of problems encountered. However, no details of individual cases will be disclosed to employers.

EMPLOYER'S CONFEDERATIONS AND ASSOCIATIONS

Irish Business Employers Confederation (IBEC)

IBEC represents the interests of the Irish business community both nationally and internationally. It has 7000 members, employing over 300,000 employees, and includes companies from every sector of employment. It represents members' interests in over eighty organisations and institutions, including the Labour Court, the Labour Relations Commission, the Employment Appeals Tribunal, FAS, the Employment Equality Agency, and the Central Review Committee. Services provided for members include employee/industrial relations, legal advice, management and training, occupational health and safety advice, stress management programs, and training in combating sexual harassment and bullying at work.

Interview with Peter Flood, Equality Officer with IBEC

'It is my job to represent employers when a case of bullying or sexual harassment is taken against one of our members. Firstly I'd have to establish the truth of the case, to ascertain its strengths and weaknesses. If an employer does not have a policy on preventing and dealing with harassment, then the fact that no complaint of harassment was ever made cannot be used as a defence in a case. If a policy does exist, and the employee never made a complaint, then there's really nothing more that the employer could have done in the circumstances. This would be accepted as a valid defence for employers by third parties. Thus, we urge all of our members to issue a policy to staff, and we offer training in how to implement the policy. We also give advice on how to carry-out an internal investigation if a complaint arises.

It is preferable that grievances be settled informally, where possible. Although the two parties involved in an Equality Officer or Labour Court hearing are never named, one can accurately guess the identity of the employer if a report of the case appears in the media (which is virtually certain to happen if the employer loses the case). This is not good for any employer.

Bullying and harassment also cause other problems for employers. Absenteeism increases. Employees are not as efficient, and not as dynamic as they can be. People tend to leave the organisation, or to be on the look-out for new jobs. Research indicates that the two main reasons why people bully others are, learned behaviour by the bully, and insecurity on the part of the bully. The latter course of bullying could arise if there is an employee who is very good at what he or she does, and his or her superior or work colleagues feel insecure because of this.

If employees are members of a recognised trade union, then I do not see any difficulties from an employer perspective if the union official is involved in the investigation. However, in practice, it can be difficult for unions to be involved in these investigations if both the victim and the alleged harasser are members of the same union, and are represented by the same union official.

There are very few cases of sexual harassment that are referred to an Equality Officer or the Labour Court. In the late '80s there would have been six or seven cases each year, but now its down to about four. If anything, an increase in cases would have been anticipated given the publicity the issue receives. Two possible reasons for this are:

1. Employers have anti-harassment procedures in place and complaints are dealt with internally rather than externally, and

2. People are more informed about the types of behaviour that are acceptable in the workplace and thus refrain from this behaviour.

Sexual harassment is definitely being dealt with by employers in a more proactive way. However there is still a lot of confusion about what constitutes sexual harassment. The Rape Crisis Centre carried out a survey some years ago, and found that a lot of managers didn't regard certain behaviour as sexual harassment unless it was physical. Managers must understand that harassment is a subjective and not an objective issue. That is, it is not whether the manager regards the issue as sexual harassment, but what the person subjected to the treatment feels. That is why training is so important.

In relation to bullying, the indications are that it is a problem in the workplace. Under the Irish Health and Safety legislation employers have a duty to protect the welfare of their employees. 'Welfare' would include issues such as stress, violence or the threat of violence in the workplace. The employer must also protect the employee who is being bullied by customers and clients.

Cases alleging bullying at work are more frequently referred under the Unfair Dismissals Act rather than the Health, Safety and Welfare Act. Because the latter Act involves attending before District, Circuit or High Court, it involves accumulating legal costs which most people are reluctant to get involved in. On the other hand under the Unfair Dismissals Acts a worker can be represented by their trade union before a Rights Commissioner or Employment Appeals Tribunal which would not involve any costs for them.

For employers to protect themselves against successful claims of bullying and sexual harassment at work, then they must:

1. Have a written policy on preventing and dealing with these issues;

2. Circulate a copy of this policy to every employee in the organisation, and

3. Train management on how to deal with the issue if it should arise.

Small Firm's Association

The Small Firm's Association is an independent constituent of IBEC. Firms with less than fifty employees usually prefer to join this association. As with IBEC, advice and assistance is offered on industrial relations and legal issues, management and training, and in the development and implementation of policies to combat sexual harassment and bullying at work.

Irish Small and Medium Enterprises Association (ISME)
Direct membership of ISME consists of over 1,500 companies, with a further 1,500 firms in the twelve organisations affiliated to ISME. 95% have started and developed their own business. They provide employment to 65,000 people. ISME provides a range of services for members, which includes advice and information on employment legislation, rates of pay, government grants and schemes, business finance, VAT, PAYE/PRSI, health and safety issues, and staff appraisal procedures.

TRAINING ORGANISATIONS

Management training
National College of Industrial Relations (NCIR)
NCIR offers a wide variety of full-time, part-time, and evening courses at certificate, diploma, degree and postgraduate level, in the areas of human resources management, industrial relations, personnel management, supervisory management, business studies, languages and related areas. Professor Joyce O'Connor is President of NCIR, and a member of the Labour Relations Commission.

'Fundamentally bullying and sexual harassment need to be tackled by advocating an ethos of equality in the workplace. Equality is not just a side issue, some theory or concept that employers and management can pay lip service to. Equality – advocating basic values, such as respect for the rights of each individual – is the main issue which needs to be addressed when discussing harassment at work.

All human relationships have the potential to be abusive. People need to be equipped with the personal coping skills to confront a bully. A code of practice needs to be established, informing staff as to which behaviours are acceptable, and which procedures to follow if they encounter a workplace bully. Up until quite recently people who were victims of bullying or sexual harassment believed they must be doing something wrong which was causing the abuse. Since this whole problem of workplace harassment has begun to come to light in the public arena, more and more people are coming forward to tell of their experiences of victimisation. It's as though these individuals have been given permission to end their silence, and to speak out. In our macho society, many men still feel too inhibited to make a complaint of harassment, particularly if the harasser is a woman. All these problems need to be discussed and addressed, so that we can begin to tip the scales in favour of the victims of workplace harassment. There is also a need for legislation to insure that workers can have union representation in cases of alleged harassment.

At NCIR our emphasis is on personal empowerment: enabling people to realise their potential. Our students are helped to develop a high level of self-confidence. The new world of work will require a workforce which is innovative, creative, flexible, continually learning and enterprising. Training in human relations and industrial relations gives students, not only a good basis for recognising and learning how to combat harassment at work, but also shows our future managers the importance of promoting good employee-management relations in the workplace. Of course training is vital in helping to raise people's awareness, and to improving their skills, at a business, technological, and human resources level. According to statistics, Irish firms spend a very small proportion of income on staff training, compared with other countries, such as Japan and the USA. Clearly, we need to place the emphasis on training, particularly in the area of human resource management.

Some of our past students have contacted the college, reporting incidents of bullying and sexual harassment at work. It can be a very harrowing and fearful experience, as the person has to deal with a dent in self-esteem as well as the fear of job loss. It helps if people can put a label on what is happening to them. Better still if the person can confront the bully, and tell him or her that this behaviour is unacceptable, and that there will be consequences if the harassment continues.

Organisations which are closed, and where bullying and harassment is condoned cannot possibly present a positive face to potential customers. When we encounter a friendly atmosphere in an office, or in a restaurant, it's not by any accident that this has occurred. A happy working environment must be promoted, developed and maintained. Employers need to become aware that people are their biggest resource. An unhappy workforce effects every facet of an organisation, from productivity to customer-relations. For those who are not motivated by any social conscience to improving conditions in the workplace, then it's a case of pure pragmatics. Research clearly shows a link between having a highly trained and happy staff, and having a successful and thriving business. There is also a strong correlation indicated between high levels of staff training, and good customer service. To remain financially viable, to be competitive and to be placed at the leading edge of our information and technological culture, businesses need to employ highly skilled and trained staff. To arrive at a situation where valuable employees are leaving their jobs because of harassment or mistreatment is counterproductive from a business point of view.

Irish businesses need to become more open by promoting good employee-management relations, by learning how to talk and how to listen to their staff. When there is open communication it makes it easier to identify problems, such as harassment, at an early stage, and to address them before they have a chance to escalate. Recent trends in business show a move away from tight hierarchical structures, towards a more loose and participative form of management. Promoting communication, team work, training, and an ethos of equality is the approach needed for any business to insure survival and growth at the dawn of the 21st century.

(A list of colleges and organisations which offer management training all over Ireland is given in 'List of organisations and useful addresses'.)

Training in combating sexual harassment and bullying
IBEC: Interview with Jenny Hayes, Management Training Executive

'When a firm decides to draw up a policy on sexual harassment and bullying in the workplace, IBEC gives advice and guidance on what to include. We advise companies on key areas such as definitions, a statement outlawing harassment, a grievance procedure, and how the disciplinary procedure operates if someone is involved in an incident of harassment. We will help them to design or to modify a proposed policy document in this area. IBEC encourages all its members to issue this policy document to their staff, to help prevent harassment from occurring, and to open up an internal channel to deal with staff complaints or grievances if harassment of any form does take place.

We then offer firms training in the prevention of sexual harassment and bullying at work. Some firms send all their managers to attend, while others just send senior management and personnel, who will then brief the next level in their organisation. The whole course takes a half day to one full day. We begin by looking at the various forms of harassment which can occur in the workplace. This usually generates a good deal of discussion as the description of what constitutes sexual harassment and bullying becomes clearer. As these programmes are run on an in-company basis, we then go on to examine the particular complaints procedure within the organisation, and train managers in the key skills when dealing with a grievance of this nature. Much of the training includes discussion, role play and a great deal of interaction enabling participants to clarify for themselves what constitutes both bullying and sexual harassment as well as how to deal with both.

Then we look at how to put the policy in place, the use of grievance and disciplinary procedures, as well as examining the kind of cases which have been recorded in the past. IBEC place an emphasis on developing the key skills of listening, questioning and non-verbal communication, as well as looking at the questions to ask and how to conduct the interview. We look at the legal side of dealing with harassment, the implications for the employer, and the channels open to an employee who wishes to take a complaint outside the company.

Irish organisations tend to be much more aware now of the importance of preventing bullying and sexual harassment at work. They are also more aware of the need to train their staff in the handling of complaints effectively. IBEC have also produced a guideline to assist employers in dealing with the whole issue of bullying at work, from introducing a policy document to raising awareness among staff members.

All IBEC members are advised of the need to have a policy in the area of bullying and sexual harassment at work. This enables employees who may have a grievance in this area to process their complaint within the organisation without undue delay. It also sends a clear signal to all employees within the organisation that harassment of any kind at work will not be tolerated. IBEC therefore advises its members to be proactive in this area by outlining the company's view on harassment at work, as well as specifying a grievance procedure for employees.'

The Rape Crisis Centre
For employers, the Rape Crisis Centre offers a comprehensive training programme for managerial and supervisory staff to assist them in coming to terms with sexual abuse in the workplace.

Within a participative framework it covers: defining the problem, investigating alleged incidents, developing appropriate policies and procedures, and legal issues.

Stress Management Training

Stress Management Institute (SMI)

The SMI offers a 50-hour certificate course in stress reduction and relaxation skills. It is aimed at health care professionals, counsellors, educators and personnel staff who wish to learn how to use and teach stress reduction and relaxation techniques, to help relieve and prevent distress. Topics include stress management techniques (such as progressive relaxation, autogenics, time management, breathing, movement awareness, self-hypnosis, yoga, coping skills, visualisations, meditation, affirmations, diet, exercise, and support systems), symptoms and diagnosis of stress, and the development of individualised stress reduction techniques. These techniques have been effective in many problems such as depression, anxiety, irritability, muscular tension, fatigue, high blood pressure, phobias, low self esteem, backaches, insomnia and cancer.

Once these techniques have been learned by one member of staff, they can be taught to staff and management and practised daily to help reduce stress at work.

Stress Prevention

Interview with Dr Richard Wynne, of the Work Research Centre

Dr Richard Wynne has worked as an occupational psychologist for seventeen years. He now works with the Work Research Centre, as a researcher, and as a stress-prevention consultant for organisations.

'My own area of research is concerned with stress and violence in the workplace. As a consultant for organisations who wish to introduce a stress-prevention program, I believe a lot of factors must be examined before an intervention is made. These include resources, management style, and the culture of the organisation. It's not a case of applying an off-the-shelf solution. I try to design a system which actually has a good chance of working.

Harassment, stress, violence, sexual harassment and bullying at work are all very complex issues. Employers are a bit loathed to grapple with them. If you happen to find there's a raving bully causing havoc in your workplace is it your responsibility? Legally of course it is. If the bullying has been covert, then it may have been extremely difficult to monitor and detect the bully's behaviour. It's a very grey area. Definitions are not clear-cut, and hence our responses are often unclear. Mostly what we hear reported are bad cases, where there's no doubt but that harassment took place. The use of words or terms can sometimes be part of the problem, hindering us from coming up with appropriate solutions. The real problem is that there are those who are grossly dissatisfied with their working environment, and their social relationships at work. There must be standards set below which no one is allowed to fall.

In Ireland, cases of sexual harassment and violence are covered, not only by employment legislation, but by criminal and civil law. In France, for example, many employees favour civil law in settling workplace disputes. The whole case rests on intent and effect. Was harassment intended, or can you bully someone without intending to? And what were the effects of the harassment? There are limits to what employers can do. People may have personal problems which they bring with them to the workplace, either making them more prone to be the harasser or the harassed. Rehabilitation programs, such as those available for people with alcohol problems, could be introduced. Then the person's job is dependent on breaking the habit – in this case bullying.

A clear-cut case of harassment is where violence is perpetrated. People have died in the course of their work. This isn't just true of those jobs involving security and policing, but includes taxi-drivers, late night shop-assistants, bank officials, and many others. In America it happens regularly. In Europe it's less frequent, but still occurs. Tom Cox, in the university of Nottingham, has done much research into violence inflicted on bar-staff. We carried out a survey for the INO recently, and this revealed that almost half of nurses had been assaulted at least once, necessitating that they take time off from work. Assaults had been perpetrated by colleagues, patients, and patient's relatives. This has been the great hidden stress factor in occupational nursing. Previous surveys in Britain had greatly underestimated the extent of the problem. There are many factors which contribute to high levels of violence in nursing: understaffing, the stress, anxiety and frustration of patients and their families who often feel out of control in these situations, working with geriatric and psychiatric patients, and the lack of training in how to prevent violence from occurring in the first place.

It's not possible to distinguish between the effects of stress, violence and harassment, in terms of the impact it has on the victim.
There can be strong emotional and physical reactions. Being bullied causes the person so much stress. Even those witnessing it
can be effected. Victims may either withdraw, collude with the
bully, or use other defensive coping strategies to try to control
the situation. Any workplace, any occupation, has the potential
to be stressful. The real issue is how is stress managed. The culture of an organisation may be very macho, and the management style may be very aggressive. This is particularly true for
blue collar firms. There may be initiation rites that new recruits
have to go through - like having practical jokes played on them.

Some work environments are more stressful due to a combina-
tion of factors: change, demand, and control. The structure of
the organisation may be changing; there's more growth and
hence more demand; workers are overloaded; quantity becomes
more important than quality; workers have no control over their
work, so they feel frustrated and trapped. No matter how much
stress managers are under, they always have some input into
decision-making. Workers who have no control over their working environment are always under the greatest stress.

If a person experiences high levels of stress, and this is sustained
over a period of time, damage will occur. Stress can occur at
work, or outside of work. Take the case of a person who has a
very heavy workload, or tight deadlines. Then a parent dies, and
the children are causing trouble at school. He develops an ulcer,
and then has a coronary. What percentage of the heart-attack is
due to his work? This causes a major problem for occupational
health, because there are other factors besides work which can
cause us health problems. Stress demands tend to go up and
down: during early adulthood stress can be very high, trying to
find a career and a relationship; people may coast in their thir-
ties and forties; then they find themselves under more stress in
their fifties, planning for retirement, and further life changes. It's
very difficult for an employer, no matter how conscientious, to
come up with ways of alleviating all forms of stress.

Most organisations introduce stress management courses, but
that places the responsibility on the individual to learn how to
cope with stress. Preventative measures at organisational level
are needed to give workers more control over their work. Other
countries, such as Denmark, Sweden and Finland, have a much

more participative approach to the problem of stress. They involve workers, consulting with them as to how work practices can be improved. In Scandinavia, occupational stress is identified by law: what it is and how it must be dealt with. Boredom can be another stress factor. Most people want some kind of stimulation or challenge in their work. New work structures may be introduced to help prevent stress: split or combined shifts, part-time work, more training for staff, and extra staffing at times of greater work-flow demands. Volvo in Sweden, for example, abolished the production line system, and set-up small work teams, where each team built the entire car. This proved to be much more satisfying for workers, as they felt they were actually achieving something.

List of organisations and useful addresses

Celtic Healing & Natural Health Clinic, 117-119 Ranelagh, Dublin 6. 01-4910689.

Centre of Personnel Development. 01-2960773.

Communication & Personal Development, 30-31 Wicklow St, Dublin 2. 01-6713636/ 6611225.

Creative Self Management, 01-8206170.

Dublin Well Woman Centre, 73 Lr Leeson St, Dublin 2. 01-6621497.

Dynamic Interpersonal Skills, Dublin 2. 01-6775655.

Foxrock Institute, Kill O' The Grange, Kill Lane, Dublin 18. 01-4939506.

(The) Irish Institute of Training, 30 Fitzwilliam Sq Upr, Dublin 2. 01-6618410.

MD Communications, 38 Spireview Lane, Off Rathgar Rd, Dublin 6. 01-4975866.

Newpark Adult Education Centre, Newtownpark Avenue, Blackrock. 01-2883725.

Personal Advancement Agency, First Floor, 117-119 Ranelagh, Dublin 6. 01-4910641.

COUNSELLING AND PSYCHOTHERAPY ORGANISATIONS

Institute of Psychosynthesis and Transpersonal Therapy, 19 Clyde Rd, Dublin 4. 01-6884687.

Institute for Reality Therapy in Ireland, 24 Glendown Court, Templeogue, Dublin 6w. 01-4562216, or 6 Red Island, Skerries, Co Dublin. 01-8491906.

Irish Association of Counselling and Therapy, 8 Cumberland Street, Dun Laoghaire, Co Dublin. 01-2300061.

Irish Association of Humanistic and Integrative Psychotherapy, 82 Upper Georges Street, Dun Laoghaire, Co Dublin. 01-2841665.

Irish Association of Hypno-analysts, Therapy House, 6 Tuckey St, Cork. 021-275785.

Irish Council for Psychotherapy, 17 Dame Court, Dublin 2. 01-6794055.

Irish Gestalt Centre, 136 Tonlegee Rd., Raheny, Dublin 3. 01-8472242.

Irish Institute of Counselling and Hypnotherapy, 118 Stillorgan Rd, Dublin 4. 01-2600118.

Irish Institute of Psychoanalytic Psychotherapy, 124 Ranelagh, Dublin 6. 01-4978896

Irish Psycho-analytical Association, 2 Belgrave Terrace, Monkstown, Co Dublin. 01-2801869/ 4967288.

EMPLOYER CONFEDERATIONS

Irish Business and Employers Confederation (IBEC), 84 Lr Baggot St, Dublin 2. 01-6601011.

Irish Small and Medium Enterprises Association (ISME), 17 Kildare St, Dublin 2. 01-6622755.

Small Firms Association, 84 Baggot St, Dublin 2. 01-6601011.

GOVERNMENT DEPARTMENTS AND INDUSTRIAL RELATIONS BODIES

Department of Justice, Equality and Law Reform, Davitt House, 65a Adelaide Rd, Dublin 2. 01-6670344.

Department of Trade, Enterprise and Employment, Kildare St, Dublin 2. 01-6765861.

Employment Appeals Tribunal, Davitt House, 65a Adelaide Rd., Dublin 2. 01-6614444.

Employment Equality Agency, 36 Upr Mount St, Dublin 2. 01-6624577.

Health and Safety Authority, Temple Court, 10 Hogan Place, Dublin 2. 01-6620400.

> Athlone: Government Buildings, Pearse St. 0902-92608.
>
> Cork: Government Buildings, 4th Floor, Sullivan's Quay. 021-961663.
>
> Drogheda: Abbey Centre, West St. 041-38536.
>
> Limerick: Government Buildings, 11-16 O'Connell St. 061-419900.
>
> Sligo: Government Offices, Cranmore Road. 071-43942.
>
> Waterford: Government Buildings, The Glen. 051-75892.

(The) Labour Court, Tom Johnson House, Haddington Rd, Dublin 4. 01-6608444.

Rights Commissioners (See Labour Court.)

MANAGEMENT TRAINING

Co Antrim

Toner Consultancy, 60 Great Victoria St, Belfast BT2 7BB. 0801232-246338.

Co Clare

ICP Consulting, ICP House, Lahinch Rd, Ennis. 065-40077.

NPI Training, Clare Business Centre, Francis St, Inch. 065-41390.

O'Neill Management Consultants Ltd., Treenduff Bohala, Claremorris. 094-84224.

Outdoor Innovations Ltd, Tinerana, Killaloe. 061-376022.

Co Cork

Academy Business Services, 12 Kilbrack In, Skehard, Blackrock. 021-294067.

Century Management, Courthouse Chambers, 27 Washington St, Cork. 021-278400.

C & I Systems Ltd, Patrick's Bridge House, 1 Patrick's Quay. 021-504155.

Conlon & Associates, Homeville Sundays Well, Cork. 021-396686.

Conway Claire Training, Cork. 021-568284.

Flexible Learning Ireland Ltd, Nicholas House, Cove St, Cork. 021-317435.

Gordon Associates, Ballyhooly Rd, Cork. 021-502723.

H-Training, Courthouse Chambers, 27 Washington St, Cork. 021-278330

ICP Consulting, 7 Bridge St, Cork. 021-507260.

Impact Training Ltd, 39 Sundays Well Rd, Cork. 021-395324.

Kenneally & Associates, Bishopstown, Cork. 021-344619.

Optima Open Learning Ltd, Killeens House, Rathpeacon, Mallow Rd, Cork. 021-301364.

Proactive Management, Walterstown, Cobh. 021-813365.

Professional Training, 24 South Bank, Crosses Green, Cork. 021-319010.

Quality Enterprise Development Ltd, The Mill, Crosses Green, Cork. 021-321041.

Thomas International Ireland Ltd, Courthouse Chambers. 021-272851.

Training Consultancy & Support Services, 46 Marlborough Ct, Cork. 021-363798.

Co Dublin

Andec Communications Ltd., 19/20 York Rd, Dun Laoghaire. 01-2807299.

Blanchard Training & Development, Brookfield House, Blackrock. 01-2833500.

Behavioural Science In Business (BSB), 64 Abberley, Killiney. 01-2825706.

Business, Finance and Technology, 4 North Georges St, Dublin 1. 01-8747024.

Century Management Ltd, Century House, U3 Newlands Park, Newlands, Dublin 22. 01-4595950.

Cadwell Consulting and Training Ltd, 7 Adelaide St, Dun Laoghaire. 01-2845008.

CKC Training International, 20 Upr Merrion St, Dublin 2. 01-6761562.

CMA Executive Training, 49 Mount St Upr, Dublin 2. 01-6766647.

College for Management Studies, Dame House, 24/26 Dame St, Dublin 2. 01-6797266.

Communiquè International, 26 Herbert Place, Dublin 2. 01-6768998.

Company Training Services Ltd, 17 Rathfarnham Rd, Dublin 6w. 01-4909114.

Converge Ltd, 12 Priory Hall, Stillorgan. 01-2880800.

Creative Management, Newcourt House, Strandville Avenue, Clontarf, Dublin 3. 01-8332281.

Delphi Training & Development, Church Lane, Rathfarnham, Dublin 14. 01-4907522.

DIT Faculty of Business, DIT Faculty of Engineering, and DIT Faculty of Tourism and Food. 01-4023000

Dublin Business School, 13/14 Aungier St, Dublin 2. 01-4751024.

Dublin City University, Glasnevin, Dublin 9. 01-7045566.

Dun Laoghaire Community College, Cumberland St. 01-2809676.

Excellence Ireland, 25 Belgrave Sq, Dublin 6. 01-4962507; also Merrion Hall, Strand Rd, Dublin 4. 01-2695255.

Executive Leadership Ireland, 21 Merrion Sq, Dublin 2. 01-6762690.

Executive Training Services, 15 Eden Park Avenue, Goatstown, Dublin 14. 01-2982825.

Export Edge Ltd, 19 Dame St, Dublin 2. 01-6778699.

Fitzpatrick Bernard & Associates, Mespil House, Sussex Rd, Dublin 4. 01-088-577349.

Form 2 Ltd, 35A Barrow St, Dublin 4. 01-6684966.

Gavigan & Associates, 15 Mount Pleasant Terrace, Dublin 6. 01-4973036.

Goodman & Associates, 5 Abbey Court, Kill O' The Grange, Blackrock. 01-2806934.

GPM Employee Resources Development, Herbert Hall, 16 Herbert St, Dublin 2. 01-6766027.

Grant Thornton Consulting Ltd, Ashford House, Tara St, Dublin 2. 01-6714677.

Grey Matters, 50 Brian Rd, Marino, Dublin 3. 01-8338732.

Griffith College, South Circular Rd, Dublin 8. 01-4545640.

Group & Interpersonal Training, 48 The Pines, Howth, Dublin 5. 01-8328016.

Hancock Peter & Co Ltd, 7 Pembroke Place, Dublin 2. 01-6761955.

Hosca Management Consultants Ltd, 5 St James Terrace, Malahide. 01-8455466.

Institute of Communication of Ireland, 50 Merrion Sq, Dublin 2. 01-6614819.

Institute of Public Administration, 57-61 Landsdowne Rd, Dublin 4. 01-6686233.

Interactive Services Ltd, U25 Phibsborough Rd, Dublin 7. 01-8600277.

International Organisational Leadership Ltd (IOL), 26 Sandyford Office Park, Dublin 18. 01-2954766.

Irish Management Institute, Sandyford Rd, Dublin 16. 01-2956911.

Jefferson Training, Jefferson House, Eglinton Rd, Dublin 4. 01-2830244.

Learning Systems International Ltd, 76A Upr Georges St, Dun Laoghaire. 01-2300044.

LSB College, Balfe House, 6-9 Balfe St, Dublin 2. 01-6794844.

MacCabe Maitiu & Associates, Cuan d'Or House, 29 Ballytore House, Dublin 14. 01-4920900.

Malahide Community School, Broomfield. 01-8463244.

Marino College, 14-20 Marino Mart, Dublin 3. 01-8332100.

McKeon Murray Business Training Services, Elm House, Leopardstown Park, Leopardstown, Dublin 18. 01-2959087/2959089.

Management & Executive Training, Jasonia House, 76 Dame St, Dublin 2. 01-4942059.

Management Research and Development Ltd, Mespil House, Sussex St, Dublin 4. 01-6688278.

MasT Ireland Ltd, 25 Adelaide St, Dun Laoghaire. 01-2800212.

Mentor Consultants, 46 Adelaide Rd, Dublin 2. 01-6615233.

Meta Concepts, 1 Marino Avenue East, Killiney. 01-2350199.

Mind Matters Ltd, 47 Leopardstown Gardens, Blackrock. 01-2783553.

Morgan Pierse, Brookfield House, Carysfort Avenue, Blackrock. 01-2833500.

National College of Industrial Relations, Sandford Rd., Ranelagh, Dublin 6. 01-4972917.

Old Bawn Community School, Tallaght, Dublin 24. 01-4520566/ 4526137.

Omega Services. 1850 222234.

Optimum Ltd, 28 Westland Sq, Pearse St, Dublin 2. 01-6779022.

Plunkett College, Swords Road, Whitehall, Dublin 9. 01-8371689.

Portobello College, Portobello House, South Richmond St, Dublin 2. 01-4755811.

Priority Management, 3 Haddington Lawn, Glenageary. 01-2846400.

Professional Development Ltd, 18 Earlsfort Terrace, Dublin 2. 01-6622867.

Promech Management Consultants, 20 Upr Merrion St, Dublin 2. 01-6762127.

Prosper Group Ltd, Hogan house, Grand Canal St, Dublin 2. 01-6613022.

RTC Tallaght, Dublin 24. 01-4042000.

Senior College, Eblana Avenue, Dun Laoghaire. 01-2800385.

Shaw Howard Training Associates Ltd, 2A Landscape Rd, Churchtown, Dublin 14. 01-28395866.

Sherry Consultants, Network House, 8 Barrow St, Dublin 4. 01-6602100.

St Finian's Community College, Castlefarm, Swords. 01-8402623.

Strategic Management Ireland Ltd, Ferrybank House, 6 Park Rd, Dun Laoghaire. 01-2845473.

Strategies Toward Success (STS) Ltd, Seafield House, Skerries Rd, Balbriggan. 01-8414700.

Teamworks, Network House, Barrow St, Dublin 4. 01-6602100.

TMI Training Consultants Ltd, 11 Priory Hall, Stillorgan, Co Dublin. 01-2784067.

Training Connections, 33 Blackthorn Green, Sandyford, Dublin 16. 01-2959013.

Training & Development Ltd, St James Court, Malahide. 01-8452933.

Trinity Institute, Temple Crescent, Blackrock. 01-2802984.

Video In Training Ltd, Zion Rd, Bushy Park Rd, Dublin 6. 01-4924992.

Videotrain International, 166 Claremont Court, Glasnevin, Dublin 11. 01-8305307.

Co Galway

Collins McNicholas Ltd, 3 Devon Place, The Crescent, Galway. 091-585358.

Foireann BDS, Cross St, Galway. 091-565277.

Speak With Ease, Furbo. 091-592462

Lilcon Associates, 21 Eyre Sq, Galway. 091-569661.

Management Performance Systems, Oranmore, Galway. 091-790637.

Petersburg Outdoor Education Centre, Clonbur. 092-46483.

Western Management Centre, Newcastle, Galway. 091-528777.

Co Kerry

Hogan Associates, Ross Rd, Killarney, 064-36454.

Co Kildare

Celtic Tacho Analysis Ltd, Tipperstown, Straffan. 01-6272392.

Moore Groome & Associates Ltd, 9 Ralph Sq, Leixlip. 01-6247004.

Co Limerick

Change Management Training, U33 Talt Business Centre, Dominic Street, Limerick. 061-314395

Clohessy Consulting, Lackyle, Ardnacrusha. 061-341511.

CVA International Ltd, 73 O'Connell St, Limerick. 061-404360.

Dantek Management and Training Consultants, 46 O'Connell St, Limerick. 061-413858.

Eglinton Personnel, 3 Michael St, Limerick. 061-312677.

Futurscope Trainers and Consultants, 64 Catherine St, Limerick. 061-314811.

Irish Business Training, Pery Court, Upper Mallow St, Limerick. 061-316177.

Lane Kelly Associates, Lock Quay, Limerick. 061-413766.

Omega Services, Curraghbridge, Adare. 061-396123.

Plassey Management and Technology Centre, University of Limerick, Plassey Technological Park, Limerick. 061-333644.

Quality Resources, Technology and Business Institute, 1 Church St, Newcastlewest. 088-638509.

Stokes Agency, The Mews, Rich hi Lisnagry. 061-331230.

Co Meath

Customer Care, Clones. 01-8252454.

Sensible Solutions, The Mayne, Clonee. 01-8251697.

Traynor & Associates, 23 Deerpark, Ashbourne. 01-8352523.

Co Waterford

Century Management, 25 Brentwood Crescent, Earscourt, Waterford. 051-852353.

Concept Services Management International, 55 Grange Heights, Waterford. 051-854737.

Coveney & Associates, Ballykinsella, Tramore. 051-381114.

Co Westmeath

W.P.H. Financial Planning Ltd, Clonbrusk, Athlone. 0902-75866.

Co Wexford

Management Resource Institute, Hospital Rd, Wexford. 053-47774.

Co Wicklow

Development Dimensions International (DDI), St Georges, Herbert Rd, Bray. 01-2866396.

Fielden House Ireland, Oaklands Putland Rd, Bray. 01-2864165.

Outdoor Dynamics, Lacken. 045-891100.

St Thomas Community College, Novara Avenue, Bray. 01-2866111.

PERSONNEL MANAGEMENT

Institute of Personnel and Development (IPD), 35 Shelbourne Rd, Dublin 4. 01-6606644.

STRESS MANAGEMENT

Academy International for Holistic & Complimentary Therapies, 48 Upr Drumcondra Rd, Dublin 9. 01-8368201.

Cathie Hogan, Blackrock, Co Dublin. 01-6600242.

Celtic Healing & Natural Health Clinic, 117-119 Ranelagh, Dublin 6. 01-4910689.

Connect Associates, Lonsdale House, Avoca Avenue, Blackrock, Co Dublin. 01-2884155.

Creative Self Management, 01-8206170.

Dublin Well Woman Centre, 73 Lr Leeson St, Dublin 2. 01-6621497.

Dynamic Interpersonal Skills, Dublin 2. 01-6775655.

Natural Living Centre, Walmer House, Raheny, Dublin 5. 01-8327859/8327861.

Personal Advancement Agency, First Floor, 117-119 Ranelagh, Dublin 6. 01-4910641.

Portobello School, Rere 40 Lower Dominick St, Dublin 1. 01-8721277.

Ross College, 66 Lr Camden St, Dublin 2. 01-4751354/ 4781991.

Stress Clinic, 13 Upper Fitzwilliam Sq, Dublin 2. 01-6611223.

Stress Management Institute (SMI), 7 Orwell Gardens, Rathgar, Dublin 6. 01-4906099.

Stress, Self-image & Confidence, 22 Rathgar Avenue, Dublin 6. 01-4921793.

STRESS PREVENTION

Work Research Centre, 22 Northumberland Rd, Dublin 4. 01-6683988.

SUPPORT FOR VICTIMS OF HARASSMENT

Anti-Bullying Unit, Trinity College, Dublin 1. 01-6772941.

Campaign Against Bullying, 72 Lakelands Avenue, Kilmacud, Stillorgan, Co Dublin.

Rape Crisis Centre, 70 Lower Leeson Street, Dublin 2. 01-6614911/6614564 Freephone: 1800778888.

TRADE UNIONS

Irish Congress of Trade Unions (ICTU), 19 Raglan Rd, Dublin 4. 01-6680641.

(Below is given a list of trade unions. All those listed are members of the ICTU, except those which are printed with an asterix before the name. For those unions which have several branches, the head office is printed first.)

Amalgamated Engineering & Electrical Union (AEEU), 5 Whitefriars, Aungier St, Dublin 2. 01-4750129

   Co. Limerick: 2 Mungret St, Limerick. 061-417311

Amalgamated Transport and General Workers Union, 55 Middle Abbey St, Dublin 1. 01-8734577/873

   Co Louth: 15 North Quay, Drogheda. 041-38953

   Francis St, Dundalk. 042-34338.

Association of First Division Civil Servants, Room 3, Graigantlet Buildings, Stoney Rd, Belfast BT4 3SX, Co Antrim.

Association of Higher Civil and Public Services, 4 Warner's Lane, Dartmouth Rd, Dublin 6. 01-6686077/ 6686064.

Association of Irish Traditional Musicians, Ballina Upr, Blackwater Town, Co Wexford.

Association of Secondary Teachers, ASTI House, Winetavern St, Dublin 8. 01-6719144.

Association of University Teachers, The Library 13G01, University of Ulster at Jordanstown, Shore Rd, Newtownanney, Co Antrim BT37 0QB.

Bakers, Food & Allied Workers Union, 80 High St, Belfast BT1 2BG.

Bakery & Food Workers Amalgamated Union, 37 Gardiner St Lr, Dublin 1. 01-8787074/ 8787978.

British Actors Equity Association, 114 Union St, Glasgow G1 3QQ.

Broadcasting Entertainment Cinematography and Thearte Union, Transport House, 1 Cathedral Rd, Cardiff, Wales CF1 9SD.

Building & Allied Trades Union, 13 Blessington St, Dublin 7. 01-8301911/ 8301280.

Co Cork: Carpenter's Hall, Fr. Matthew Quay, Cork. 021-276728.

Chartered Society of Physiothearpy, Physiotherapy Dept, Royal Victoria Hospital, Grosvenor Rd, Belfast BT12 6BA.

Civil Service Alliance, 'Castleville', Carrigoran, New-market-on-Fergus, Co Clare.

Communications Workers Union, 575 North Circular Rd, Dublin 1. 01-8366388.

Cork Operatives Butchers' Society, 55 North Main St, Cork. 021-504151.

Electricity Supply Board Officers' Association, 43 East James Place, Lower Baggot St, Dublin 2. 01-6767444.

Federated Union of Government Employees, 32 Parnell Sq, Dublin 1. 01-8787057.

Fire Brigades' Union, 40 Cloona Crescent, Belfast BT17 HG.

GMB, 3-4 Donegal Quay, Belfast BT1 3EA. 0801232-312111.

Graphic Paper & Media Union, Graphic House, 107 Clonskeagh Rd, Dublin 6. 01-2697788

Co Cork: 69 Shandon St, Cork. 021-300333

Co Kildare: 1 Crofton Court, New Ross, Naas. 045-879270.

Guinness Staff Association, St. James Gate, Dublin 8. 01-4536700.

Institution of Professionals, Managers and Specialists, 75-79 York Rd, London ES1 7AQ.

Irish Air Line Pilot's Association, Corballis Park, Dublin Airport, Co Dublin. 01-8444900.

Irish Bank Officials Association, 93 St. Stephen's Green, Dublin 2. 01-8722255.

* Irish Distributive & Administration Trade Union, Killoran House, Catherine St, Limerick. 061-314648.

Irish Federation of Musicians and Associated Professions, 63 Lower Gardiner St, Dublin 1. 01-8744645.

Irish Federation of University Teachers, 11 Merrion Sq, Dublin 2. 01-6610910/ 6610909.

Irish Medical Organisation, 10 Fitzwilliam Place, Dublin 2. 01-6767273.

Irish Municipal, Public and Civil Trade Union, Nerney's Court, Dublin 1. 01-8745588.

Irish National Teacher's Organisation (INTO), 35 Parnell Sq, Dublin 1. 01-8722533.

* Irish National Printers & Decorators Trades Union, 76 Aungier St, Dublin 2. 01-4751720.

Irish Nurses Organisation (INO), 11 Fitzwilliam Place, Dublin 2. 01-6760137.

* Irish Postmasters Union, 35 Fitzwilliam Place, Dublin 2. 01-6760260
   Co Waterford: Kilmeaden. 051-384224.

Irish Print Union, 35 Gardiner St Lr, Dublin 1. 01-8743662/ 8747320.

Irish Veterinary Union, 32 Kenilworth Sq, Dublin 6. 01-4971160.

Mandate Union of Retail, Bar and Administrative Workers, 9 Cavendish Row, Dublin 1. 01-8746321
   Co Cork: IBS House, 1 Emmet Place, Cork. 021-270101
   Co Galway: Hynes Building, St Augustine St. 091-562750.
   Co Waterford: 36 Michael St. 051-874631.

Manufacturing Science Finance Union (MSF), 15 Merrion Square, Dublin 2. 01-6761213
   Co Limerick: Hartstonge St. 061-310244.

Marine Port & General Workers Union, 14 Gardiner Place, Dublin 1. 01-8726566.

National Association of Probation Officers, 45 Tobarcooran Avenue, Glengormley, Newtownabbey, Co Antrim.

National Association of Schoolmasters and Union of Women Teachers, 5 Carneybaun Drive, Portrush, Co Antrim. 0801265-822704.

National Association of Teachers in Further and Higher Education, 411 Lisburn Rd, Belfast BT9 7AP 0801232-618288.

* National Bus & Rail Union, 54 Parnell Sq, Dublin 1. 01-8730434.

National League of the Blind of Ireland, 21 Hill St, Dublin 1. 01-8742792.

* National Taxi Union of Ireland, 76 Thomas St, Dublin 8. 01-4537220.

National Union of Insurance Workers, 4 Glendermere Heights, Newtownabbey, Co Antrim BT36 6QZ.

National Union of Journalists (NUJ), 8th Floor, Liberty Hall, Dublin 1. 01-8741207/ 8748694.

National Union of Knitwear, Footwear and Apparel Trades, 55 New Walk, Leicester, England LE1 7EB.

National Union of Rail, Maritime and Transport Workers, 19 Bellisk Park, Cushendall, Co Antrim.

National Union of Sheet Metal Workers of Ireland, 6 Gardiner Row, Dublin 1. 01-8745701.

Northern Ireland Musician's Association, 3rd Floor, Unit 4, Fortwilliam Business Park, Dargan Rd, Belfast BT3 9JZ.

Northern Ireland Public Service Alliance, 54 Wellington Park, Belfast BT9 6BZ.

Operative Plasterers and Allied Trades Society of Ireland, Arus Hibernia, 13 Blessington St, Dublin 7. 01-8304270.

Prison Officer's Association, 18 Merrion Sq, Dublin 2. 01-6625495/7678501.

Public Service Executive Union, 30 Merrion Sq, Dublin 2. 01-6767271.

Public and Commerical Services Union, c/o HMIT, Ballymena, Kilpatrick House, High St, Ballymena, Co. Antrim BT43 6DR. 0801266-633033.

Sales Marketing & Administrative Union of Ireland, 37 Gardiner St Lr, Dublin 1. 01-8787070.

Seamen's Union of Ireland, 61 North Strand Rd, Dublin 3. 01-8363500.

Services Industrial Professional Technical Union (SIPTU), Liberty Hall, Dublin 1. 01-8749731

    Co Carlow: Barrack St, Carlow. 0503-31251

    Co Cavan: Farnham St. 049-31419

    Co Cork: Connolly Hall, Lapps Quay, Cork. 021-277466

        Cobh: 021-813340

        Liberty Hall, Fair St, Mallow. 021-21493

        Connolly Hall, Connolly St, Middleton. 021-613276

    Co Donegal: Church St, Buncrana. 077-62573

    Co Galway: 25 Salthill Lr. 091-522188

    Co Kildare: Hibernian House, Leinster St, Athy: 0507-78390

        Edward St, Droichead Nua. 045-432318

    Co Kilkenny: 8 Dean St, Kilkenny. 056-61668

    Co Laois: Main St, Portarlington. 0502-21899

    Co Limerick: U4 Church St, St. Johns Square. 061-317289

    Co Longford: 23 Ballymahon St. 043-45247

    Co Louth: Palace St, Drogheda 041-37462

        St Crispin Hall, Seatown, Dundalk. 042-34243

    Co Meath: Danshaw Ctr, Common Rd, Navan. 046-29437

    Co Monaghan: The Diamond. 047-82953

    Co Offaly: Bridge St, Tullamore. 0506-21163

        Unity Hall, Church St, Tullamore. 0506-21157

    Co.Tipperary: New Quay, Clonmel. 052-22987

    Co Waterford: Connolly Hall, Summerhill, Waterford. 051-874773

    Co Westmeath: Bishopsgate St, Mullingar. 044-40490

    Co Wexford: Corish Memorial Hall, Wexford. 053-22848

    Co Wicklow: Bradshaw's Lane, Arklow. 0402-32562.

Teachers Union of Ireland, 73 Orwell St, Rathgar, Dublin 6. 01-4922588/ 4922510.

Technical, Engineering & Electrical Union, 5 Cavendish Row, Dublin 1. 01-8747047/8722369

    Co Cork: Old Fire House, 23 Sullivan's Quay, Cork. 021-319033/319036

    Limerick: Mechanics Institute, Hartstong St. 061-319669.

Transport Salaried Staffs' Association, Nerney's Court, Off Temple St, Dublin 1. 01-8743467.

Union of Construction, Allied Trades and Technicians (UCATT), 56 Parnell Sq, Dublin 1. 01-8731599

    Co Cork: 6 Fr Matthew Quay, Cork. 021-272174.

* Union of Motor Trade Employees, 16 Inns Court, Wine Tavern St, Christchurch, Dublin 8. 01-6779803.

Union of Shop, Dristributive and Allied Workers, 40 Wellington Park, Belfast BT9 6DN. 0801232-663773.

UNISON, Unit 4, Fortwilliam Business Park, Dargan Rd, Belfast BT3 9JZ. 0801232-770813.

Veterinary Officer's Association, 4 Warner's Lane, Dartmouth Rd, Dublin 6. 01-6686077/ 6686064.

Text References

Argyle, Michael, *Social psychology of work*, Penguin, London, 1989.

BBC, *Bullying at work: Combating offensive behaviours in the workplace*, BBC for business, London (Text and Videos).

Beck, A., & Willis, A., 'Trouble in store', *Police Review*, 11 January, 1991.

Blennerhassett, Evelyne, & Gorman, Patricia, *Absenteeism in the Public Service: Information Systems and Control Strategies*, Institute of Public Administration, Dublin, 1986.

Chadwick-Jones, J., Nicholson, N., and Brown C., *Social psychology of absenteeism*, Praeger, New York, 1982.

Gunnigle, Patrick, Flood, Patrick, Morley, Michael & Turner, Thomas, *Continuity and change in Irish employee relations*, Oak Tree Press, in association with the Graduate school, UCD, Dublin, 1994.

Home office Statistical Bulletin, Notifiable offences – England and Wales, Issue 9/93, Government Statistical Service, 1993.

Iaffaldano, M.T., and Muchinsky, P.M., 'Job satisfaction and job performance: A meta-analysis', *Psychological Bulletin*, 97, 251-73, 1985.

Johnson, RH, Ryan, AM, and Schmit, MJ, 'Employee attitudes and branch performance at Ford Motor Credit', in Rotchford N (Chair), *Linking employee survey data to organisational outcome measures, Practitioner forum conducted at the Ninth Annual Conference of the Society of Industrial and Organisational Psychology*, Nashville, Tennessee, USA, (April) 1994.

Likert, Rensis, *New patterns of management*, McGraw Hill, New York.

Maslow, Abraham, *Motivation and Personality*, Harper & Row, New York.

Mayo, Elton, *The human problems of an industrial civilisation*, Macmillan, New York, 1933.

McGregor, Douglas, *The human side of enterprise*, McGraw Hill, New York.

Mowday, R.T, Porter, L.W., and Steers, R.M., *Employee-organisations linkages*, Academic Press, New York, 1982.

O'Connell, P., 'Violence and vandalism in general practice', *Irish Medical Times*, Dublin, 1994.

Petty, M.M., McGee, G.W., and Cavender, J.W., 'A meta-analysis of the relationships between individual job satisfaction and individual performance', *Academy of Management Review*, 9, 712-21.

Poster E., & Ryan, J, 'At risk of assault', *Nursing Times*, 9 June, 89, 23, 30-33, 1993.

Reynolds, P., *Dealing with crime and agression at work: A handbook for organisational action*, McGraw-Hill, London, 1994.

Schlesinger, LA, and Zornitsky, J., 'Job satisfaction, service capability, and customer satisfaction: An examination of linkages and management implications', *Human Resource Planning*, 14, 141-150, 1991.

Schneider, B, and Bowen, DE, 'Personnel/human resources management in the service sector', *Personnel and Human Resources Management,* 10, 1-30, 1992.

Shanahan, Kate, *Crimes worse than death,* Attic Press, Dublin, 1992.

Wahl, K., Robbery, 'Violence and threats in the financial sector in the Nordic countries', *FIET, Tackling violence at work,* 23-25, 1994.

Wynne, Richard, Clarkin, Nadia, & Cox, Tom, *Guidance on the prevention of violence at work: Draft Report* , Work Research Centre, 1995.

Zimbardo, P., 'Transforming experimental research into advocacy for social change', in M. Deutsch and H. Hornstein (eds), *Applying social psychology,* Lawrence Erlbaum, Hillsdale NJ, 1975.

The Advisory Committee on management training, The Stationery Office, Government Publications, Dublin, 1988.

Bullying in the workplace: Guidelines for action, ICTU.

Employment Equality Agency, *Annual Report* (1993, 94, 95, 96), Dublin.

Equal Opportunities Commission For Northern Ireland, *Sexual harassment at work: Guidance on prevention and procedures for deaing with the problem,* Belfast, Oct.ober1993.

FORCE FAS, *Company training in Ireland,* Planning and Research, FÁS, Dublin 1995.

Human Resource Development (White paper), Government Publications, Dublin 1997.

IBEC: *Guideline Number 19: Bullying/Harassment in the workplace.*

IBEC Periodicals: *Workplace Bullying: A variation of harassment* (IR Databank – human resources, Vol 14, Issue 237, IBEC, Dublin, Feb. 1996.

IBEC: *Guideline 4 : Dealing with sexual harassment in the workplace,* March 1996.

IBEC: *The Law on Sexual Harassment.*

IPD: *Key Facts: Harassment at work,* IPD House, Camp Road, London SW19 4UX.

OECD Economic Surveys 1995, Ireland, page 85.

Report European Commission Seminar: *Sexual harassment at work: On the protection of the dignity of women and men at work,* Ineke M. de Urnes, The Hague, 7, 8, 9 November 1991.

July 96-June 97 Statisitics & Financial Summary, Rape Crisis Centre, Dublin, 1997.

The Labour Court's Annual Report (1996), Government Publications, Dublin, 1996.

Violence at work, Health and Safety Authority, Dublin.

Workplace stress: Cause, effects, control, Health and Safety Authority, Dublin, 1997.

Further Reading

Adams, Andrea, *Bullying at work: How to confront and overcome it*, Virago Press, London, 1992.

Byrne, Brendan, *Bullying: A community approach*, The Columba Press, Dublin, 1997.

Gaudry, Eric, & Spielberger, Charles D., *Personal power: Use, misuse and abuse*, Harper Collins, Victoria, 1995.

Glasser, William, *The quality school*, Harper & Row, New York, 1990.

Hart, Archibald D., *The crazy-making workplace*, Highland, Surrey, 1993.

Harvey, Noel, *Effective supervisory management in Ireland*, NCIR Press, Dublin, 1994.

Harvey, Noel, & Twomey, Adrian F., *Sexual harassment in the workplace*, Oak Tree Press, Dublin, 1995.

Higgins, Eddie, & Keher, Nuala, *Your rights at work*, Institute of Public Administration, Dublin 1996.

O'Donnell, Vivette, *Bullying: A resource guide for parents and teachers*, Attic Press, 1995.

Pringle, Rosemary, *Secretaries talk: sexuality, power and work*, Verso, London, 1989.

Randall, Peter, Adult *Bullying: Perpetrators and Victims*, Routledge, London, 1997.

Redman, Warren, *Counselling your staff*, Kogan Press, London, 1995.

Summerfield, Jenny, & Van Oudtshoorn, Lyn, *Counselling in the workplace*, Institute of Personnel Development, London, 1995.

Whitymer, Claude, *Mindfulness and meaningful work: Explorations in right livelihood*, Parallax Press, California, 1994.

Wright, Lesley, & Smye, Marti, *Corporate Abuse*, Simon and Schuster, London, 1997.

Wylie, Peter, and Grothe, Mandy, *Dealing with difficult colleagues: How to improve troubled business relationships*, Piatkus, London, 1996.

Bullying, intimidation, harassment in the workplace, SIPTU, Dublin.

Employee Relations information service: Sexual harassment and bullying at work, IBEC, Dublin.

Sexual harassment and dignity at work: Gender equality in employment ', Employment Equality Agency, Dublin.

Sexual harassment is no joke, SIPTU, Dublin.